HOFFA'S CONNECTION

The Story of Sylvia Pagano: the Kansas City Girl at the Center of the Mafia's Alliance with the Teamsters Union

BY

FRANK R. HAYDE

3

TABLE OF CONTENTS

AUTHOR'S NOTES

In writing this book, I was extremely fortunate to work with researcher extraordinaire, Patrick J. Fasl, of Kansas City, Missouri. Pat specializes in uncovering new information and solving mysteries. Pat captured my attention with his first book, *John the Yegg*, which closed the case of the infamous 1946 election in Kansas City. His second work, *The Syndicate and the Police*, is a case study in urban corruption and another invaluable contribution to Kansas City history. Throughout this project, Pat was a joy to work with, and if his friendship is all I gain from it, the effort will have been well worthwhile.

Names that appear in all capital letters i.e. SYLVIA, indicate an excerpt from an official FBI document, usually a summary of a recorded conversation.

Various synonyms for "Mafia" appear this book including LCN (La Cosa Nostra); mob; Outfit; Company; syndicate; secret society etc. *"Borgata"* is used synonymously with "family" to indicate a local branch of the national syndicate.

Most of the quotes attributed to Sylvia's son, Chuckie O'Brien, come from Jack Goldsmith's book, *In Hoffa's Shadow*.

DEDICATION

To my wife, Julie, with love and gratitude.

INTRODUCTION

In 2013, Harvard law professor Jack Goldsmith contacted me after he read my book, *The Mafia and the Machine: The Story of the Kansas City Mob*. In addition to his Harvard credentials, Goldsmith is also a former Assistant U.S. Attorney General and senior fellow at the Hoover Institution who rose from humble circumstances. But for me, the most fascinating thing about Jack Goldsmith is that he is the stepson of Chuckie O'Brien. And for those who don't know, Chuckie O'Brien was the leading suspect in the disappearance of Jimmy Hoffa.

When Goldsmith contacted me, he was working on his book, *In Hoffa's Shadow: A Stepfather, a Disappearance in Detroit, and My Search for the Truth*. Goldsmith wanted to know if I had uncovered any information on Chuckie's family in my research for *The Mafia and the Machine*, because, Goldsmith told me, Chuckie was from Kansas City.

"*What!?* Chuckie O'Brien was from Kansas City?" My flattery at being contacted by someone of Goldsmith's stature turned to embarrassment for not knowing this fact. I had often said that a connection to the Hoffa case was about the only thing missing from the epic story of the KC Mob. I was somewhat comforted by the fact that none of the other chroniclers of the Kansas City Mafia whose books and films followed *The Mafia and the Machine* seemed to have known this either; O'Brien is absent in every treatment of the story. Despite Chuckie's national notoriety, his KC roots were deeply buried and scarcely known.

Suffice to say, Goldsmith wrote a stellar book with little help from me. When I finally read *In Hoffa's Shadow*, I was blown away by the content, but especially the parts concerning Chuckie O'Brien's mother, Sylvia Pagano, the Kansas City girl who introduced Jimmy Hoffa to the Mafia.

But Goldsmith's book is about Chuckie, not Sylvia. This book attempts to build on what Goldsmith published about Sylvia and to interpret the connections between Sylvia and some of the most consequential people and events in the history of organized crime and organized labor. Prior to Goldsmith's book, Pagano's name had been briefly mentioned and often misspelled in various volumes on Jimmy Hoffa, but only in the form of a cursory and usually misleading sentence or two. But Sylvia's life is yet another chapter in the inexhaustible saga of the American crime syndicate. Historians have yet to fill in all the gaps in the endlessly interconnected world of *La Cosa Nostra,* but Sylvia's story brings us one step closer, and it offers a rare example of a woman who cracked the glass ceiling in the exclusively male world of the Mafia.

Sylvia was a behind-the-scenes force, and records of her relatively short life—she was 56 when she died—are scarce compared to those of the high-profile and well-documented men she influenced. Sylvia was completely committed to the code of silence that so many mafiosi strayed from. She guarded her secrets, kept her mouth shut, and left little to posterity. Photographs of Sylvia are few and often grainy; a testament to her mysterious life of secrecy.

But from a storyteller's perspective, Sylvia's significance is less about biographical details than it is the connections that are unique to her. Through her life, we can link people and places and events that make up a veritable cross-section of Mafia history. Our exploration of her life led to familiar territory but also into some unexplored rabbit holes that hid missing pieces of the Mafia puzzle.

CHAPTER ONE

A BRIEF INTRODUCTION TO JIMMY HOFFA

"The teamsters union is the most powerful institution in this country aside from the United States government itself. In many metro areas the Teamsters control all transportation…the Teamsters drive the trucks that clothe and feed us and provide the vital necessities of life…Quite literally your life—the life of every person in the United States—is in the hands of Hoffa and his Teamsters."

Robert F. Kennedy, 1960

In his prime, James Riddle Hoffa was an American celebrity, appearing twice on the cover of Time Magazine in the late 1950's while wielding gargantuan power as the President of the International Brotherhood of Teamsters (IBT).

A hero to many and a villain to just as many, Hoffa grew the Teamsters into the largest labor union in the country. Under Hoffa, the Teamsters had over two-million members and enough leverage to shut down the American economy with a trucking strike. Hoffa negotiated enviable pay and benefits for his members, and most rank-and-file Teamsters revered him. He was a working-class guy himself, and he was as tough as they came.

Jimmy Hoffa became practically synonymous with the Mafia, but Hoffa was never a member of *that* international brotherhood, and despite the vowel at the end of his name, Hoffa wasn't even Italian.

Of German and Irish ancestry, he hailed from small town Indiana; a "peckerwood"[1] from a poor and hardscrabble coal-mining background. After his father died when Jimmy was seven years old, the Hoffa's moved to Detroit, where industry flourished and jobs were plentiful.

Hoffa dropped out of school at age 14 and went to work in warehouses and on loading docks. When the labor wars heated up in the 1930's, Hoffa discovered he had a knack for organizing workers. He spent much of the decade on the frontlines of violent strikes and picket lines, cracking heads and getting his own head cracked. The young man had the charisma to lead others into battle, and he was fearless even when outnumbered. "I've never met anyone with his charisma," said Hoffa's lawyer, Frank Ragano. "He had leadership qualities that could make men follow him off a cliff."

Hoffa's dedication to unionism was matched by a herculean work ethic and unchecked ambition, and he climbed the ranks of organized labor with speed and ruthlessness. For Hoffa, the ends justified the means, and thanks to Sylvia Pagano, the means included a basket-tight association with the Mafia.

Sylvia's Mafia connections helped Hoffa rise to the top but also drew the attention of the ambitious brother of the

---

[1] The term "peckerwood" was commonly used to describe a country boy from rural or small-town America with no obvious ethnic background.

soon-to-be President of the United States. In his role as a Justice Department lawyer investigating labor racketeering, Robert F. Kennedy grilled Hoffa in a series of congressional hearings that became highly personal for the two stubborn men. They became sworn enemies, with Kennedy labeling Hoffa "the most dangerous man in the country," and Hoffa deriding Kennedy as a "spoiled brat."

The heat on Hoffa increased after John F. Kennedy was elected President and appointed his brother as Attorney General. Hoffa spent much of the early 1960's fighting the prosecutorial efforts of Robert Kennedy's "Get Hoffa" squad. The younger Kennedy brother seethed as Hoffa won a string of acquittals and taunted Kennedy for his inability to win a conviction. In 1962 Kennedy brought Hoffa to trial on charges of extortion and bribery. During the trial, a mentally unstable man with a pellet gun fired shots at Hoffa. Hoffa's loyal minion, Chuckie O'Brien, sprang into action and pummeled the assailant. O'Brien was Sylvia Pagano's son and Hoffa's most trusted associate. His instinctually violent defense of his boss reflected the absolute dedication O'Brien had for his hero and surrogate father.

Sylvia's son, Chuckie O'Brien (R), backs-up his surrogate father, Jimmy Hoffa, at the height of Hoffa's power in the early 1960's.

When President John F. Kennedy was assassinated in 1963, Hoffa was observed celebrating. When virtually every flag in the country was flying at half-staff after the assassination, Hoffa ordered the flag at Teamsters

Headquarters in Washington D.C. to be raised back up to full mast. With his motives, money, and connections to other suspects, Hoffa has often been pegged by informed sources as having been part of a conspiracy to kill President Kennedy.

But if Hoffa thought the President's death would keep him out of prison, he was wrong. In 1964, he was convicted in two separate cases and sentenced to 13 years in federal prison. Among his fellow prisoners was a notorious Teamsters boss and New Jersey mafioso named Anthony "Tony Pro" Provenzano. Tony Pro was one of many powerful mobsters whose relationship with Jimmy Hoffa was initiated and facilitated by Sylvia Pagano. Sylvia had made close allies out of Hoffa and Provenzano, but tensions between the two old friends flared in prison, and Sylvia's two dear friends became bitter enemies.

After President Nixon granted him an early release from prison, Hoffa set about regaining control of the IBT. This did not sit well with the Mafia, who found Hoffa's successor, Frank Fitzsimmons, even more pliable to their wishes than Hoffa had been. But Hoffa would stop at nothing to get his union back. He even threatened to expose Fitzsimmons' web of Mafia corruption. The crime syndicate was also concerned about Hoffa's scheduled appearance before a U.S. Senate committee that was investigating both the Kennedy assassination and a Mafia/CIA conspiracy to assassinate Cuban dictator Fidel Castro.

On July 30, 1975, Hoffa left his home in Detroit for an ostensible meeting with Sylvia's old friend Tony Provenzano and her long-time lover, Detroit crime boss Anthony "Tony Jack" Giacalone. Jimmy Hoffa was never seen again. His disappearance only enhanced his notoriety, and it spawned an obsessive and still-active search for Hoffa's remains and the truth about who killed him.

Several gangsters have taken false credit for the historic hit, but the man who the FBI pointed to as the leading suspect in Hoffa's disappearance took his denials to his grave. That man was Sylvia Pagano's son, Chuckie O'Brien, whose Irish surname obscures a Mafia legacy that traces through his mother back to people and places distant from her days as Hoffa's connection. To grasp the full context of Sylvia's legacy and its impact on Jimmy Hoffa, it is necessary to first travel back in time to a momentous murder in the most remote and forgotten of Mafia strongholds: Pueblo, Colorado.

CHAPTER TWO

PUEBLO AND THE LEGACY OF THE SCAGLIA BROTHERS

"Pellegrino Scaglia was killed following a noisy argument which brought a split in the family of Pueblo, Colorado. In the struggle many young men fell."

Nicola Gentile, writing from Sicily in 1963

Pellegrino Scaglia arrived in Pueblo with a face full of scars. They represented a few of the 43 stab wounds two assailants had inflicted on him in the "Dago Hill"[2] neighborhood of St. Louis, Missouri in March 1911.

But Scaglia was not a man to be pitied. The attack on him mirrored his own violent ways. The Scaglia and Cardinale families had been engaged in a feud that dated back to when both families lived in the village of Burgio in the Agrigento Province of Sicily. The feud escalated in New York after friends of the Cardinales were targeted for extortion by Pellegrino Scaglia and his associates in the "Black Hand," the network of Sicilian extortionists that later morphed into the more modern American Mafia during Prohibition in the 1920's.

---

[2] "Dago Hill" was the term used in articles about Scaglia in the *New York Times* and *St. Louis Post Dispatch* in 1911.

Black Hand letters usually demanded money from other Sicilians and threatened death if their demands were denied. Black ink handprints and drawings of daggers dripping with blood decorated the dreaded messages. Large communities of honest Sicilians were terrorized as *La Mano Nero* made good on their threats to kill letter recipients or their family members.[3] Pellegrino Scaglia was a typical Black Hander, which is to say he was a diabolical and dangerous man.

But Giuseppe Cardinale was not afraid of Scaglia. At a meeting of a Brooklyn benevolent society in 1908, Cardinale confronted Scaglia over the attempted extortion of his friends and allegedly slapped Scaglia in the face—a universal affront, but to a Sicilian man like Pellegrino Scaglia, an instant vendetta.

A few months later, Giuseppi Cardinale cautiously accepted Pellegrino Scaglia's invitation to take a walk and sort out their differences. Cardinale's worried wife waited for him to return home, but he never did. Giuseppi Cardinale was found hours later on a bench in Coffey Park, Brooklyn, stabbed to death.

After swearing vengeance on Pellegrino Scaglia, Giuseppi's uncle, Giovanni Cardinale, received a Black Hand letter. "You'll be killed at the window," it said.

---

[3] One of the darkest examples of Black Hand violence occurred in 1919 in Kansas City, where an eight-year-old boy named Frank Carramusa was murdered after his father could not pay the amount the extortionists had demanded.

On January 18, 1909, a man with a slug-loaded shotgun made good on the threat, shooting and killing Giovanni Cardinale through a rear window of his Brooklyn home.

Pellegrino Scaglia disappeared from New York and was not heard from until March 1911, when he was found in the gutter in St. Louis' "Dago Hill" neighborhood with 43 stab wounds—12 in the face and neck. The crime was thought to be the work of the Cardinales, but Scaglia refused to say. "It's all right," he told police. "It's my affair and I'll get him."

With a will to live nourished by a lust for vengeance, Scaglia did not even wait until he was fully healed before returning to Brooklyn.

On July 30, 1911, Giuseppi Cardinale's brother, Bartholdi Cardinale, worked late at his barbershop. He arrived home at midnight, climbed the stairs to his second-story flat, and fell into his chair. While his wife removed his shoes, a gunman took aim from the recently rented second-story apartment across the street. The double-barreled blasts woke the neighborhood. Like his uncle Giovanni, Bartholdi Cardinale was murdered through a window of his home. Witnesses reported seeing a scar-faced man resembling Pellegrino Scaglia in the area in the days leading up to the shooting and exiting the building immediately afterwards.

The last remaining Cardinale brother, Vincenzo, told the New York Times, "The hand that slew all the others will get me yet. It's only a question of time. I know that my death warrant is signed."

Scaglia was arrested in St. Louis, extradited to New York, and tried for murder. Vincenzo Cardinale's blood must have run cold when Scaglia was acquitted. Fortunately for

Vincenzo, Scaglia decided to search for greener pastures in Colorado.

Sylvia's relative, Pellegrino Scaglia

Pueblo might have been a long way from the eastern urban power bases of the secret society, but it eclipsed Denver in syndicate clout and was more like Sicily than any of the Little Italy's in America's principal cities. On the horizons were mountains and the old rural adobe Catholicism of the same Spaniards who had once conquered Sicily. Here, the mafiosi rode horses and planted crops. Some wore overalls and carried dirt under their fingernails, remaining truer to their peasant roots than their silk-suited, manicured brethren in the bigger cities. Like their fathers and grandfathers in Sicily, the hardcore mafiosi of Southern Colorado fought battles in fields and creeks with the same shotguns they used to hunt pheasant.

Pellegrino Scaglia had connections in Pueblo, including his younger brother, Mariano Scaglia. Most of the town's Sicilians came from the Scaglia's home province of Agrigento. Pellegrino had changed his name to Tony Viola, but the local Black Handers knew better. Here was the man who had crawled back from the edge of death, completed his vendetta, and beat prosecution. Pellegrino Scaglia was welcomed into the Pueblo Mafia as a leading "man of respect."

With his wife and three children, Scaglia made a home at 904 Elm Street. His brother Mariano, who would later become influential in Sylvia Pagano's life, lived on the same block and ran a barbershop at 205 North Union Avenue. The Scaglia brothers developed a close association with a physically frail but educated mafioso named Vincenzo Chiapetta. Mariano Scaglia was married to Mary Campo, who was a cousin to the wives of Vincenzo Chiapetta and his brother Pietro, who had married two sisters—an arrangement not uncommon among Italians of the time. In another Italian familial custom, Pellegrino and Mariano Scaglia gave the same names to their children; they both had sons named Phillip and daughters named Anna Marie. Mary Campo and the Chiapetta women had close family ties to Kansas City, where a young Sylvia Pagano would later become close to her Aunt Mary and her uncle, Mariano Scaglia.

Pellegrino opened a grocery store next to his house. When Colorado outlawed liquor in 1916—three years ahead of national Prohibition—the Scaglia brothers became some of the Mafia's earliest bootleggers as they sold booze out of the store. Pellegrino also opened a pool hall on Elm Street that became another outlet for liquor and a meeting place for fellow mafiosi, who now admired Scaglia's earning power along with his much-revered ruthlessness. By the time Prohibition spread to the rest of the United States, Pellegrino Scaglia, with his brother Mariano by his side, was thought by many in Southern Colorado to be the boss of the Pueblo Family.

The Scaglia brothers' illegal liquor came from the Carlino brothers, former farmers who now used their barns for booze. The Scaglias enjoyed a close relationship with the Carlinos, and Pellegrino's wife, Marie, was godmother to one of Pete Carlino's sons. Competing with the Carlinos in the bootlegging racket was another family of farmers, the D'Annas.[4] Bad blood between the two families was beginning to boil, and the D'Annas knew that Pellegrino Scaglia was the Carlino's strongest ally.

On May 6, 1922, Pellegrino Scaglia was driving his horse-drawn grocery wagon along East Mesa Avenue past St. Mary's Church. Riding with him were his four-year-old daughter, Anna Marie, and a nine-year-old neighbor boy named Frank Cordaro. A Dodge touring car with curtained windows approached and shotguns blasted. Scaglia might have lunged for the loaded revolver under his seat but instead threw himself over his daughter. Young Frank Cordaro, fatally hit with buckshot, fell from the wagon and was crushed underneath it. Anna Marie Scaglia survived, traumatized, and covered in her father's blood. Pellegrino Scaglia was dead at the age of 38.

---

4 Also spelled "Danna."

Frank Cordaro's parents later had another son whom they named Frank in memory of their firstborn.

Scaglia's killing sparked a split in the Pueblo Family and a bloody, eight-year war between the Carlino and D'Anna factions, but there were other ramifications that were not revealed until 41 years later, when a transnational mafioso named Nicola Gentile wrote his Italian-language memoirs in Agrigento, Sicily.

Nicola Gentile had a unique role in the Mafia as a travelling diplomat whose specialty was staying executions. He split his career between Sicily and the United States, where at different times he was a member of at least 6 different *borgatas* including the Mangano Family in New York and the families in Philadelphia, Pittsburg, Cleveland, San Francisco, and Kansas City. Gentile had also spent time in Pueblo and was close to Vincenzo Chiapetta.

Nicola Gentile. His 1963 memoirs were not published in English, but FBI agents scoured the content and got a crash course in the history and ways of the secret society.

According to Gentile, Pellegrino Scaglia's murder and its aftermath caused Scaglia's closest family members and allies to flee Pueblo and seek refuge in Kansas City under "the protection of the local *capo*." Pellegrino Scaglia's wife and children, his brother Mariano Scaglia, father-in-law Frank Accomondo, nephew Luca Colletti, and cousins by marriage Vincenzo and Pietro Chiapetta made up the band of refugees.

Each of these men brought with them wives, children, and other family members in a mini diaspora from Pueblo to Kansas City.

According to Gentile, "a man named LaRocca" formally objected to Kansas City's protection of Scaglia, Accomondo, and Colletti, whom LaRocca charged with committing unsanctioned killings in the wake of Pellegrino's murder. Frank LaRocca was a KC mobster and Agrigento man whose sister, Leonardo Soldano, lived in Pueblo. The unsanctioned killings LaRocca objected to can be deduced as the hits on John and Carl Mulay, close friends of LaRocca who were ambushed in retaliation for Pellegrino Scaglia's killing.[5]

Nicola Gentile represented the accused Puebloans as the case was appealed to the highest levels of Mafia power in New York. Toto D'Aquila, the boss of bosses at the time, presided over an assembly concerning the fate of men from these two far-flung families. Just when a death sentence seemed imminent, the tribunal was moved to Pittsburgh, where Nicola Gentile finally convinced the higher powers to spare the Puebloans lives. 30 years later, the FBI would still claim that organized crime was local and provincial, but the Pellegrino Scaglia saga illustrates how interconnected the network was even in the days of the Black Hand.

Pellegrino Scaglia was a one-man Mafia microcosm. The events of his life and death trace the evolution, methods,

---

[5] John Mulay was gunned down 9 months after Pellegrino Scaglia as he stepped out of a street car at Evans and Mesa Avenues in Pueblo. Four months later, while sitting in his car, Carl Mulay survived a shooting that claimed the life of his passenger, Vincenzo Urso.

pathos, and geographical span of the American Mafia from Sicily to New York, St. Louis, Pueblo, and finally, Kansas City, where the influx of Agrigentons from Pueblo would stamp the values of the subculture onto Sylvia Pagano and her son, Chuckie O'Brien. The Chiapetta brothers' wives were Silvia's cousins, but it was Sylvia's uncle, Mariano Scaglia—Pellegrino Scaglia's brother and underboss—who would grow close to Sylvia and provide her with an entrée into the orbit of *La Cosa Nostra*. In due time, Sylvia Pagano would carry the Scaglia torch to Detroit and spread its flames to Jimmy Hoffa, who would ignite a conflagration that engulfed the nation.

CHAPTER THREE

KANSAS CITY

"It should be noted that O'Brien had been Binaggio's chauffer prior to his entry into the U.S. Armed Forces in the early 1940's"

FBI memo by Special Agent John L. Shelburne
6/12/1963

Thanks to the diplomatic efforts of Nicola Gentile at the assemblies in New York and Pittsburgh, Mariano Scaglia and the other accused Puebloans were spared the death penalty but stripped of formal membership in the secret society. Luca Colletti returned to Colorado and Frank Accomondo ended up in Houston. Mariano Scaglia stayed in Kansas City, where he would become influential in Sylvia's life and coexist with his accuser, Frank LaRocca, who operated the LaRocca Wholesale Grocery in KC's Little Italy.[6]

---

[6] LaRocca maintained ties to Colorado through his sister's family and other associates in Pueblo. In 1937, Jennie Mulay, the 22-year-old daughter of unsanctioned Pueblo murder victim John Mulay, died in Kansas City while visiting the LaRoccas. 20 years later, an elderly LaRocca made two trips to Gunnison, Colorado where he purchased 13 revolvers at Elmer's Sporting Goods. In 1960, one of those guns was found near the scene of the attempted murder of Kenneth Sheetz, a burglar who had testified against Anthony Biase, the rackets boss of Omaha, Nebraska. Sheetz was shot four times, but he survived and identified KC gangsters Felix Ferina and Anthony "Tiger" Cardarella as his assailants. Frank LaRocca was later convicted of lying to a grand jury about his purchase of the guns.

Frank LaRocca. His grocery was a fixture in Sylvia's North End neighborhood for decades.

Sylvia's other relative, Vincenzo Chiapetta, had dodged LaRocca's accusations in the unsanctioned killings in Pueblo, but not long after the migration to Kansas City, Chiapetta was sentenced to death by Los Angeles boss Vito DiGiorgio for alleged transgressions that had occurred years earlier in New Orleans. The leadership of the KC *Borgata* again called on Nicola Gentile to travel to California to represent Chiapetta and the interests of the KC Family. With the help of Rosario DeSimone, a Pueblo transplant whose son would later lead the LA Family, Gentile again prevailed, and Chiapetta was cleared with his credentials intact. Chiapetta went on to flourish in Kansas City, partnering with the DiGiovanni brothers and other top KC mafiosi in the "Sugarhouse Syndicate," which consolidated illegal liquor and other rackets in KC during Prohibition. After repeal, Chiapetta partnered with the

DiGiovannis and John Blando in Superior Wine & Liquor, a lucrative and longstanding business with exclusive distribution rights for Schenley products.

Vincenzo Chiapetta, the Puebloan transplant to Kansas City whose wife was cousin to Sylvia, tries to block journalists from photographing his face.

Having been stripped of his status as a "made man," Mariano Scaglia was not entitled to the privileges and status enjoyed by LaRocca and Chiapetta, but the brother of Pellegrino Scaglia had friends in the KC Family and he was hardly shunned. His businesses and family relations show that he remained well-connected and respected despite his controversial demotion. His connections included members of his wife's family. Scaglia's wife, Mary Campo, was the sister of Sylvia Pagano's mother, Maggie Campo Pagano.

Sylvia was 9 years old when her relatives arrived from Pueblo. She was born August 9, 1914, to Maggie Campo Pagano and her husband Joseph Pagano, another Agrigento man who hailed from the same village as Frank LaRocca. The Pagano's lived in the heart of KC's Little Italy at 522 East 5th street, right next-door to the family of Pueblo refugee Pietro Chiapetta, and just down the street from the LaRocca Grocery. When Sylvia was born, her parents were still heartbroken over the infancy death of their first daughter, whom they had named Sylvia. Like the parents of young Frank Cordaro, who was killed with Pellegrino Scaglia in Pueblo, the Pagano's gave the name of their deceased child to their new one. The choice of names honored their departed daughter's memory and helped them heal, but it would cause Sylvia a major problem 50 years later.

Had her Uncle Scaglia stayed in Colorado, Sylvia Pagano might have ended up more like most of Kansas City's honest and law-abiding Sicilians. Sylvia would later say that her father had done a little bootlegging during Prohibition, but her parents seem to have been hardworking, solid citizens with no criminal records. Joseph Pagano was a track inspector for the Kansas City streetcar and Maggie was a seamstress at Woolf Brothers Clothing Company. Sylvia's two brothers, Mario and Paul, later served in the Navy and Marines respectively. Paul eventually ran a dancing school in KC while Mario became an engineer in Columbus, Ohio.

Then again, this was the North End of Kansas City, where Mafia influence permeated. The maternal side of Sylvia's family, the Campos, had crime connections even before Mariano Scaglia married into the family.

The name Campo has been absent in the annuls of organized crime in Kansas City, but according to Sylvia's son, Chuckie O'Brien, the family name carried clout that went back to the old country. Sylvia's maternal grandfather, Paolo Campo, was identified by O'Brien as a cheesemaker and a mediator between Sicilian *borgatas*. "My great-grandfather had a tremendous reputation of honor," O'Brien told his stepson.

Other Campo's were also involved in the rackets. Three of Sylvia's uncles, Salvatore, Dante, and William Campo, were arrested in 1927 in connection with the robbery of the J.P. Gilman Granite Company. Two years later, Willie Campo was nearly killed during a 1929 robbery at a sugar distributing facility. Willie later affiliated himself with Joe Lusco, the KC racketeer who challenged Johnny Lazia for political control in the bloody election of 1934. With his own outlaw history, Mariano Scaglia seems to have fit in well with his Campo in-laws, and the maternal lineage might have been a factor in Sylvia taking a path that her brothers avoided.

By the 1920's, KC's North End was no longer the slum it had been a generation earlier, but many families still lived in the type of grinding poverty that made a decent pair of shoes a luxury for a child. Nice clothing was a status symbol, and Sylvia benefited from her mother's skills as a seamstress at Woolf Brothers, one of the finest clothiers in the Midwest. Chuckie O'Brien told of his mother growing up wearing dresses custom made by her mother. But stylish clothes were not the only thing that made Sylvia pop on the streets of Little Italy. At some point, the comely girl got the nickname, *"Facci,"* Italian for "face." With her lustrous black hair, expressive brown eyes, pinchable cheeks, and winning smile, Sylvia was easy to take a shine to, and she won the hearts of protective men like her Uncle Mariano Scaglia. Lectures on virtue, respect, and the sanctity of the family included a strong emphasis on loyalty and *Omerta*: the ability to keep one's mouth shut and guard secrets. Sylvia absorbed such lessons and obeyed them in a manner that instilled trust and admiration in the patriarchs of her extended family.

Less significant than the education Sylvia received in the ways and customs of her Sicilian neighborhood was the formal schooling she received at Emerson Elementary and Manual Training High School. Sylvia's attendance was poor, and her grades below average. She is not listed as having graduated from Manual High, and the only mention of Sylvia in the school's yearbooks is a 1931 entry that lists her as a member of the "Date Committee," which operated alongside the Decoration and Refreshment committees in the facilitation of the school's social events.

Bringing people together seems to have been a natural calling for the sociable Sylvia, but when it came to her own dating, she eschewed the student body for her own neighborhood, where she caught the eye of a service station attendant named Charles Linton O'Brien.

Mystery and misinformation surround the man who would become Sylvia's first husband and the father of her only child. Jimmy Hoffa said that Chuckie O'Brien was the son of a Detroit union organizer named Frank O'Brien who died on a picket line when Chuckie was a child. An organized crime investigator in Detroit said that Chuckie's father might have been one Sam Scaradino, whose parentage would ostensibly make Chuckie a full-blooded Italian.

But for decades, many observers believed Jimmy Hoffa was Chuckie's father. Dan Moldea, the most prolific and persistent of Hoffa journalists, wrote, "O'Brien was generally considered by Teamsters officials, underworld figures, and government agents to be Hoffa's real son." Chuckie resented the rumors that he was born out of wedlock: "I'm not a bastard. I've got a father. My mother was not some kind of goddamn prostitute; she was a saint…But if I had a father, I couldn't have asked for a better one [than Hoffa]. He was the only father I've ever had."

Far less is known of Chuckie's real father than his surrogate one, but one thing about Charles Linton O'Brien is clear: he had criminal tendencies to rival Pellegrino Scaglia.

Charles O'Brien was born on June 28, 1910, in St. Louis, Missouri, the son and namesake of a boilermaker with roots in Cork County, Ireland. He began his criminal career at age five, when he was arrested for stealing a neighbor's horse and buggy. Charles's father died around the same time Charles dropped out of school after the 4th grade. Charles spent the rest of his boyhood as a street urchin, racking-up dozens of arrests and earning the nickname "Bunny," a possible reference to his small stature and impressive agility. Later, friends would call him "Bing," a reference to crooner Bing Crosby and a compliment to O'Brien's fine singing voice.

On December 6, 1925, 15-year-old Charles O'Brien went off the rails. O'Brien would later confess that on that night he and five companions, including his 19-year-old brother, Frank O'Brien, had "drunk some home brew before starting out to rob."

They found their targets sitting in a Packard automobile on the 5500 block of Pershing Ave in St. Louis. The robbers drew pistols and forced the chauffeur into the backseat with the owner of the car and his niece. Three of the hoodlums got into the Packard and drove their victims to an alley, where they robbed them of 25 dollars and their Packard. The three thieves then picked up the other three co-conspirators.

Charles O'Brien—the youngest of the bunch—was behind the wheel of the Packard when two policemen stopped them for speeding. Officer Theodore Funke, unaware of the earlier crimes, got in the front seat of the Packard next to Charles and told him to drive to the Magnolia Avenue police station while the other officer followed in the squad car. A block and a half later, according to Officer Funke, someone in the backseat shouted, "Let him have it!" Funke turned around and saw Frank O'Brien pointing a revolver at him. In the ensuing chaos, Officer Funke was shot seven times before Charles stopped the car and kicked the policeman to the curb. O'Brien floored the gas as the officer in the squad car opened fire on the Packard. O'Brien crashed through the lowered gates of a railroad crossing and careened onto Grand Avenue, where he crashed into another car, injuring the driver and three of the six gangbangers in the Packard.

Charles and Frank O'Brien fled the scene and hid out in Chicago until Christmas Eve, when they were captured returning to their St. Louis home at 4200 Easton Ave. Charles was remanded to the boys' house of detention where he fell in with a crew of Irish and Sicilian boys. On January 24, 1926, Charles and five of his pals assaulted a trustee and a guard, stole the guard's keys, and escaped. Charles's sister turned him in the next day.

Officer Theodore Funke

Officer Funke survived his seven gunshot wounds and testified against his assailants, most of whom were over 18 and received long prison sentences. Frank O'Brien got 25 years. 15-year-old Charles was sentenced to five years in the Reform School for Boys in Boonville, Missouri, a penal institution described as "a hellhole, a viper's nest, and a study in sadism."

Boonville was also fertile recruitment ground for the mob. Charles picked up some rudimentary Sicilian while he was incarcerated, and he absorbed some of the same cultural lessons learned by his future wife, Sylvia Pagano. Shortly before his release in 1930 at age 20, the quick-with-his-fists young man was recruited to Kansas City. "My father was a tough little motherfucker," said Chuckie O'Brien. "He would put your lights out in two seconds, and that's why they sent him to Kansas City."

With Tom Pendergast and Johnny Lazia in control, Kansas City in 1930 offered plenty of opportunity for aspiring gangsters, but only if they had connections. Charles O'Brien was fortunate enough to be sponsored by a rising star in the national crime syndicate: Charlie Binaggio.

Binaggio was only 21 years old in 1930, but he was already assembling his own crew and expanding his operations into Colorado, where he developed a relationship with Denver's Smaldone brothers that eventually led to a partnership in Central City gambling operations. But ties with Colorado were only the beginning. Charlie Binaggio would eventually earn the admiration and investment dollars of Mafia dons in New York, Chicago, and other large cities. For Charles O'Brien, Binaggio represented status and opportunity.

A 1963 FBI report describes Charles O'Brien as having worked as Binaggio's chauffeur. It was a plumb position that immersed O'Brien in the underworld, schooled him in the rackets, and introduced him to most of the mafiosi in the city, including Binaggio's powerful pal, Paolo "Frankie Three Fingers" Coppola. The job also demanded other duties besides driving. "My father was protecting Binaggio," said Chuckie. "He was a bodyguard. He was a shooter. And a driver."

Sylvia's husband's boss, Charlie Binaggio, pictured in the late 1940's

Chuckie's father was also an attendant at a Binaggio-controlled service station located along Sylvia Pagano's walking path between the North End and Manual High.[7] Charles was four years older than Sylvia and charming enough for the teenage girl to fall in love with. Sylvia's family seems to have disapproved of their *Facci's* relationship with a wild and crazy

---

[7] Manual High was located on East Truman Road between Tracy and Forest Avenues.

Irishman, for the couple eloped to nearby Cass County for a Justice of the Peace marriage. Sylvia was not pregnant when she married O'Brien in November 1932 at the age of 18; their son Chuckie was born 13 months later, on December 20, 1933. According to Chuckie, he was baptized at St. Patrick's Cathedral at 8th and Cherry Streets in downtown Kansas City. Baptismal documents are unavailable, but Chuckie claimed that his godfather was Charlie Binaggio. Considering the O'Briens' relationship with Binaggio, and the natural choice he would have been for Sylvia and her husband, it's a credible claim.

Around the time Chuckie was born, members of Sylvia's extended family joined the flow of Italians making the short move from the North End to the Northeast. Sylvia, Charles, and Chuckie spent the rest of the 1930's living with Sylvia's parents in a duplex at 3223 Independence Avenue. Next door at 3225 was another duplex occupied by Mariano Scaglia's family and Phil Lascuola, who was known on the streets as Phil School.

With her aunt and uncle living next door, Sylvia remained under the influence and tutelage of Pellegrino's Scaglia's brother and underboss. Chuckie O'Brien said that Mariano Scaglia was a "big man" in KC during Prohibition. The members of the Sugarhouse Syndicate might have begged to differ, but Scaglia's immediate entry into the post-Prohibition, legal-but-still-mob-controlled KC liquor business effectively proves his bona-fides as a former bootlegger who operated with the crime family's blessing. In the 1930's, Scaglia had several licensed establishments. Scaglia Liquors was located two doors down from the family compound on Independence Avenue. In the heart of the 18th and Vine jazz district, Scaglia owned two Hey-Day liquor stores and the Hey-Day Night Club, all of which employed and served a largely African American clientele.

Sylvia's uncles Dante and Willie Campo and her cousin, Phil Scaglia, all worked for Uncle Mariano at Hey-Day. Phil, who lived under Mariano's roof and was the same age as Sylvia, was sometimes confused with his double cousin, Pellegrino's son Phil, who later opened the Golden Nugget night club at 3832 Main Street. Pellegrino's son eventually served 16 years as a Democrat representing the 30th District[8] in the Missouri House of Representatives. Sylvia's other cousin—— Mariano's son, Paul Scaglia—married Carolina Lococo, the daughter of Gaetano Lococo, who was one of the "Five Iron Men," or Mafia captains who reigned over the rackets in KC.

Phil School's presence at Mariano Scaglia's address is another illustration of Scaglia's connections and Sylvia's proximity. Phil and two of his four brothers, Mike and Joe Lascuola, were stalwarts of the KC Outfit whose activities spanned the gamut of rackets. In 1931, Phil was arrested with Charlie Binaggio and others after a liquor raid by local cops and federal agents at Joe Lusco's flower shop at 1039 Independence Avenue. The raid turned into a deadly shootout in the darkened second story of the building, where one agent and one bootlegger were killed in an exchange of gunfire that has been attributed to the legendary fugitive outlaw Charles "Pretty Boy" Floyd.[9]

---

[8] 47th to 63rd between Paseo and Prospect

[9] If it was in fact Floyd who killed the agent that day, he escaped. But Floyd would hide out in Kansas City again in the days leading up to the Union Station Massacre in 1933.

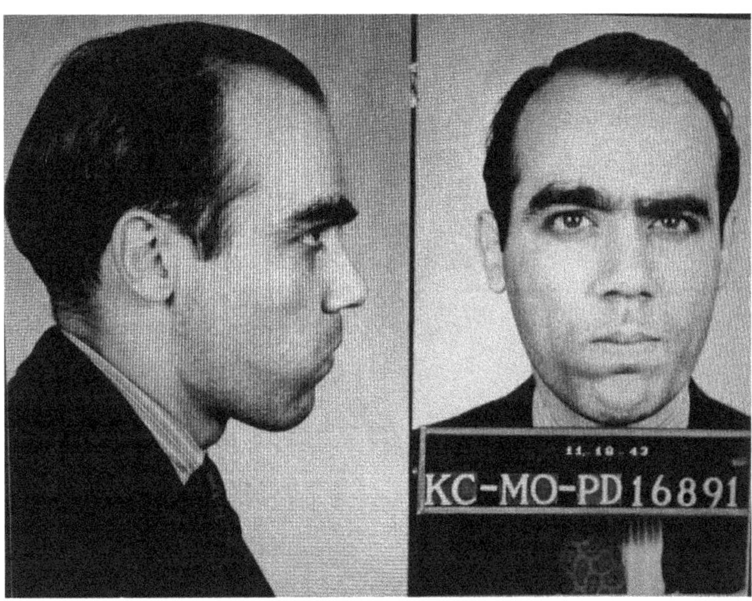

Sylvia's next-door neighbor, Phil Lascoula in a 1943 mugshot

Phil School was also charged along with Carl "Cork" Civella and three other men in the February 27, 1934, broad-daylight robbery and murder of bank messenger Webster Kemner at the corner of Ninth and Walnut Streets. The killers made off with $206,294 in securities—approximately $5 million in 2026 dollars. The charges against Lascuola, Civella, and Meyer "Ace" Berman were eventually dismissed for lack of witness testimony. Cork Civella would later act as underboss to his brother, Nick Civella, who became the nationally recognized face of organized crime in Kansas City as he led the Family's ventures into the Teamsters Union and Las Vegas casinos.

Carl "Cork" Civella's mugshot from 1934

Nick Civella's mugshot from the mid-1940's.

Considering their addresses and ages, Phil Lascuola seems as likely as anyone in Sylvia's tight clique of Binaggio associates to have introduced Sylvia to the Civella brothers. Regardless, Sylvia knew the Civellas well, and her son Chuckie referred to them as "Uncle Nick and Uncle Cork." Chuckie also spoke of having a similar hometown relationship with William "Willie the Rat" Cammisano.

1940 was the last year that census records listed Sylvia, Charles, and Chuckie living on Independence Avenue. When Charles registered for the draft in February of 1941, he listed Sylvia's mother, Maggie Pagano, as the person who would always know his address. Charles initially listed the Kay Hotel at 816 Main Street as his residence, but on Feb 17, 1941, that address was crossed out and replaced with 1024 West 70th Street—the home of his boss and the godfather of his son, Charlie Binaggio.

O'Brien's break from the duplex on Independence Avenue marked the end of his marriage to Sylvia. Charles would soon leave for the Army and serve only one year before being honorably discharged, but he never returned to Kansas City and Chuckie never saw his father again. It left a void in Chuckie's life that Jimmy Hoffa would soon fill.

Charles O'Brien's departure also seems to have left a void in the life of Charlie Binaggio. Shortly after his chauffeur's exit, Binaggio crashed his car into a pedestrian and killed him. Binaggio was charged with manslaughter, but a coroner's jury ruled it an accident with no criminal liability.

After his discharge from the Army, Charles O'Brien went to work for a racketeer named Jerome Knoll in California. Knoll was a convicted bookmaker who owned a service station in Beverly Hills. O'Brien's work at the service station included helping Knoll run a black-market scheme where they sold new cars without an agency license.

On June 2, 1947, Jerome Knoll entered Charles O'Brien's apartment at 427 Shirley Place and found his employee hanged to death. Charles's death was ruled a suicide.

Chuckie O'Brien, already scarred by his father's abandonment, was humiliated by what he considered to be his father's sinful and unmanly death. He told anyone who asked that his father had been murdered on a picket line. Later, he admitted that his father had been found hanged, but claimed it was murder for transgressions committed against some of Charlie Binaggio's colleagues back in Kansas City.

At the time of his former driver's death, Binaggio was reaching the peak of underworld power and prestige. By 1949, he had leveraged his political prowess and the ruthless efficiency of the Kansas City Crime Family to become the brightest star in the whole national syndicate. But Charlie's luck changed quickly. In 1950 he was sensationally killed with his lieutenant, Charles Gargotta, in a politically charged double murder inside a Democratic Party club on Truman Road. Like the double murder of Pellegrino Scaglia and young Frank Cordaro in Pueblo 28 years earlier, the double murder at the Democratic club was a historical turning point with far-reaching consequences. 25 years later, Binaggio's godson, Chuckie O'Brien, would be implicated in yet another epochal killing.

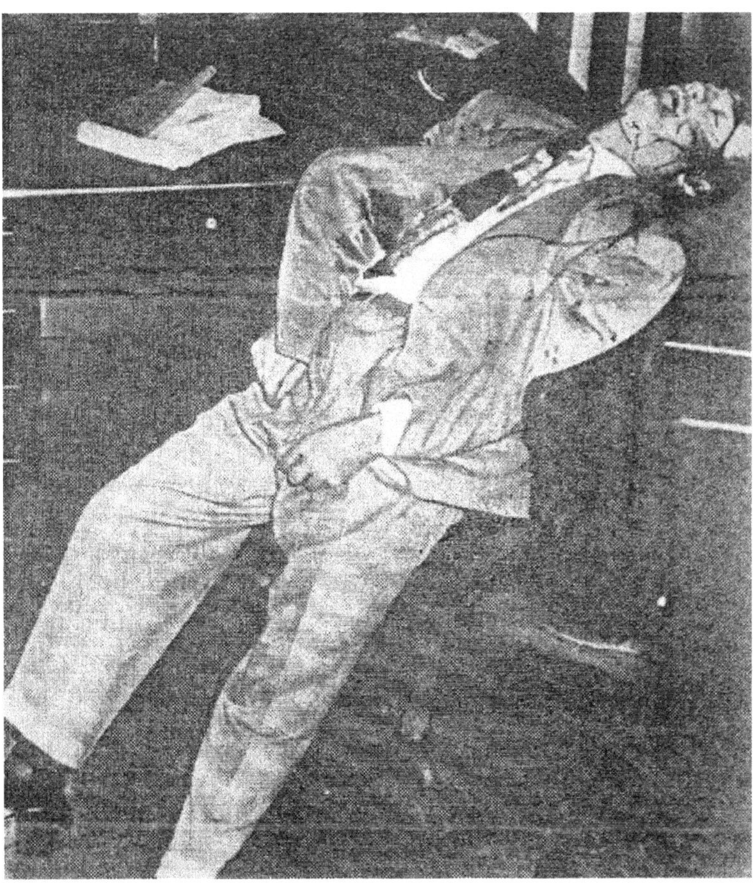

Charlie Binaggio after the double murder at the Democratic club in Kansas City. The politically charged killing spawned the historic Kefauver congressional investigation into organized crime.

CHAPTER FOUR

DETROIT

"They trusted her. They knew that my mother was strong and never opened her mouth about anything."

Chuckie O'Brien

Sylvia decided to leave Kansas City as her marriage to Charles O'Brien fell apart in 1940. Sylvia was 25 years old and Chuckie was seven when they made plans to move to Detroit. Sylvia's Uncle, Dante Campo, had moved there and would shelter Sylvia and Chuckie when they arrived. According to Chuckie, Uncle Mariano Scaglia got Sylvia an office job at a produce terminal in Detroit's Eastern Market run by William "Black Bill" Tocco, the original godfather of the Detroit Mafia.

Sylvia's first employer in Detroit, William "Black Bill" Tocco

As Sylvia's closest familial connection to older mafiosi, Uncle Mariano might well have helped facilitate Sylvia's welcome in Detroit, but the connection to Black Bill Tocco seems more likely to have been Frank Coppola, whom Detroit investigators believed was having an affair with Sylvia during her early days in Detroit. Sylvia seems certain to have known "Frankie Three Fingers" Coppola in Kansas City, and to have arrived in Detroit on his arm. Unlike Uncle Mariano, who had been stripped of membership, Coppola was well positioned to ask a favor from Don Tocco. Coppola was from the same part of Sicily as Tocco, and he knew Black Bill well. Coppola was on record as being in the produce business in Detroit at the time, and he appears likely to have been partners with Tocco in the business where Sylvia worked.

Like Nicola Gentile, Frank Coppola was an international mystery man with memberships in multiple families in the United States and Italy. He had lost the ring and pinky fingers of his left-hand sometime before he fled Italy in 1926 as a fugitive wanted for murder. Coppola spent the 1930's bouncing between Detroit, Los Angeles, St. Louis, Chicago, and Kansas City, where he was close to James Balestrere, Tony Gizzo, and Charlie Binaggio.

Coppola used a different pseudonym in every town, but his high-ranking status followed his short stature—he was only 5'2" —wherever he went. Like Nicola Gentile, Coppola was a roving emissary, advisor, arbitrator, and judge. He built lucrative partnerships with some of the top made men in the country, including New York's Frank Costello and Charlie Binaggio in Kansas City. As a close friend of Binaggio, Coppola would have gotten to know Charles O'Brien, and Sylvia, too. Coppola's timeline shows him leaving KC and returning to Detroit during the same period Sylvia moved there. An FBI memo from 1963 states that Sylvia had once worked in a bar owned by Frank Coppola. As one of the most well-connected mafiosi in the country, Coppola helped put Sylvia on the fast-track to friendship with the upper echelon of La Cosa Nostra in Detroit and beyond.

Sylvia's boyfriend Paolo "Frankie Three Fingers" Coppola

Sylvia arrived in Detroit on the brink of America's involvement in World War II, but as ground zero in the labor battles of the Great Depression, the capitol of industrial unionism was already a war zone of its own. Strikes and picket lines were ubiquitous and often violent. Unions battled with company goons, scabs, police, and each other in melees filled with tear gas, firehoses, rocks, bats, bombs, and bullets. "During my first year as an organizer I'd had my scalp laid open six times wide enough to need stitches," said Jimmy Hoffa. "I'd been beaten up by police, company guards, goons, and strikebreakers two dozen times in one year. My brother Billy had been shot in the stomach by a company official and I'd seen a union business agent beaten to death by company goons."

Santo "Cockeyed Sam" Perrone, who was another one of Sylvia's early contacts in Detroit, personified the goons Hoffa spoke of. An impulsively violent and much-feared man, Perrone was one of Detroit's most aggressive strikebreakers and union busters. As partners in the Detroit Michigan Stove Works plant, Santo and his brother Gaspare waged a decade-long, police-protected campaign of intimidation and terror against organizers and sympathizers of the United Autoworkers Union. In 1948 and '49 respectively, UAW President Walter Reuther and his brother, Victor Reuther, were both shot and badly injured inside their own homes by assailants firing shotguns through their windows a'la' Pellegrino Scaglia. One of the getaway drivers later confessed and implicated Cockeyed Sam as having ordered the Reuther hits.[10]

---

[10] Perrone and his crew beat the charges when the witness fled to Canada and corrupt elements of Detroit law enforcement sabotaged the case. The police detective in charge of the case went to work for the Detroit Teamsters after he was dismissed from the department.

One of Sylvia's early Detroit LCN contacts, Santo "Cockeyed Sam" Perrone

Santo Perrone's antiunion sentiments were typical of the Detroit Family at the time. With Sylvia's help, that would soon change, but for now, local gangsters were making good money working for employers as strikebreakers, and business owners like Black Jack Tocco generally rejected union representation and the higher wages and stricter regulations that went with it. Organizing workers at mob run companies was dangerous business, but organizers were a tough lot, and just as some gangsters became union men, some union men became gangsters. They had a lot in common, after all, including an affinity for Sylvia Pagano. Two of Sylvia's early admirers from her time working at Tocco's were Teamster Bert Brennan and gangster Anthony Giacalone.

Bert Brennan's rise in the Teamsters Union was contemporaneous with Jimmy Hoffa's, and he was Hoffa's closest collaborator until his death in 1961. During the labor wars of the 1930's, Brennan was arrested four times for bombings and twice for assault. Robert Kennedy described Bert Brennan as, "a wiry, muscular, little man with close-cropped hair. He always looks healthy and tanned-and mean, He talks tough; he acts tough. An incessant smoker, he has a habit of biting a cigarette between his front teeth (just like the movie badmen), curling his lips back and talking while keeping his cigarette perfectly in place."

Anthony "Tony Jack" Giacalone was four years younger than Sylvia but already making a name for himself as feared enforcer and heavy-hitting strikebreaker. Tony Jack's brother, Vito "Billy Jack" Giacalone was to his older brother what Bert Brennan was to Jimmy Hoffa. The Giacalone brothers' rise in the crime syndicate would track Hoffa and Brennan's rise in the Teamsters, but in 1940, the two pairs of young men were on opposite sides of Detroit's ongoing labor wars.

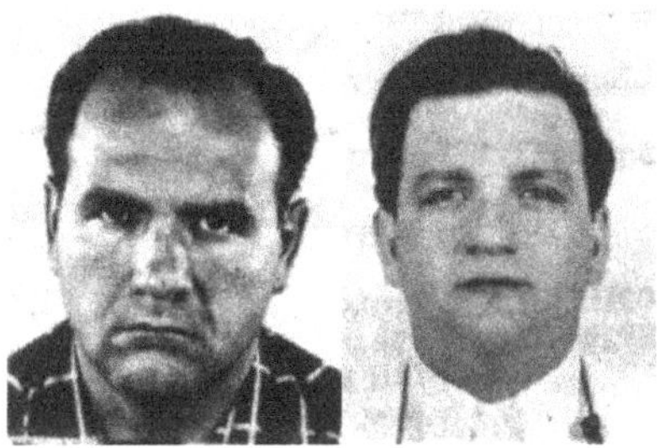

L to R: Anthony "Tony Jack" Giacalone and his brother, Vito "Billy Jack" Giacalone

Bridging the two sides was Sylvia Pagano, who left Tocco's produce company to work for Bert Brennan and the Teamsters. Among her early assignments was "salting," the union tactic of sneaking representatives into ordinary jobs where they would undertake their real objective: recruiting workers into the union. "My mother would get a job in the bakery, in A&P and Kroger's, or in a potato chip factory, and start signing people up," said Chuckie O'Brien. It was difficult, even dangerous work, but Sylvia proved her mettle and gained the respect of her fellow organizers who admired her loyalty and persistence.

Most written accounts of Jimmy Hoffa have him meeting Sylvia almost a decade before he actually did. The notion that Hoffa met Sylvia in the early 1930's allowed for the myth that Hoffa and Sylvia had an affair that produced Chuckie O'Brien, but for all the misinformation that surrounds Sylvia and Hoffa's relationship, reliable investigators were all but unanimous in listing Sylvia Pagano as the person who facilitated the relationship between Jimmy Hoffa and the Mafia—one of the most notorious and storied alliances in American history and the source of our most renowned unsolved murder mystery.

It began as a diplomatic coup that made allies out of adversaries amid a monthslong Teamsters-led strike of the Detroit Lumber Company in 1941. Scab truck drivers, backed by a crew of company-paid gangsters led by Tony Giacalone, were breaching the picket lines. "Uncle Tony was young and they were kicking the shit out of the strikers and bringing the trucks out," said Sylvia's son.

The stakes for Hoffa were high. Teamster rivals in the Congress of Industrial Organizations—a federation of unions that would later merge with the American Federation of Labor into the AFL/CIO—were exploiting the unrest by backing a union that was poaching Teamsters drivers as part of the CIO's plan to crush the Teamsters into oblivion. When a Teamster picket named Arthur Queasbarth was killed by a brick thrown at his head, Hoffa felt the existence of his union and his very livelihood was at stake if he couldn't turn the tide and settle the strike. "He knew that the only way he could win was to get an army together," said Chuckie O'Brien, "But he didn't have the financial money to buy people."

According to O'Brien, Bert Brennan told Hoffa he should, "talk to *Facci*."

Brennan knew that Sylvia could make men melt. It wasn't just her sex appeal. She had that, but so too did every typical mob moll. Sylvia was different. She showed respect and commanded respect. She was wise in their ways and she worked hard. Sylvia could be trusted; not only to keep her mouth shut, but to reliably carry out assignments, grant favors, and get results. Men who normally excluded women from their business affairs welcomed Sylvia's opinions and ideas. "She was a lady, but she was tough," said her son. "And whatever it would take to get it done, she would do it. In those days, most women were intimidated. She wasn't—I don't care who it was. If she had to do something, if somebody asked her to do something, she wasn't suicidal, but she'd get the job done."

Chuckie O'Brien's stepson, Jack Goldsmith, offered a tidy summary of the Sylvia he came to know through conversations with her son and other family members: "She was smart, charming and resourceful," Goldsmith wrote. "But her defining characteristic—one she developed during her years married to Chuckie's father—was her grit."

Facci **in 1957**

Hoffa took Brennan's advice and talked to *Facci*. Sylvia set up a meeting between Hoffa and three key members of the Detroit Family: her beau, Frank Coppola; strikebreaker Santo Perrone; and Angelo Meli, whose nephew, Vince Meli, would later become godfather to Sylvia's granddaughter. Before the introduction, Sylvia schooled Hoffa in how to act with the mafiosi. "Being a hillbilly, he thought all that Italian shit was poky-dory," said Sylvia's son. "He didn't understand all the formalities and all that, he thought it was all bullshit."

The meeting resulted in Tony Giacalone's crew switching sides. This put Hoffa in league with the very men who, according to Chuckie O'Brien, threw the brick that killed Teamster Arthur Queasbarth. A Detroit Lumber representative described the turmoil the company faced from the new alliance: "At least 60 trucks have been wrecked, and assaults have been made upon may of our drivers. These hoodlums have been cutting tires, breaking windshields, wrecking motors and otherwise interfering with lumber deliveries."

In lieu of cash, Hoffa allowed the occasional scab truck to exit, setting the drivers up to be hijacked by the Giacalone crew. "When you got a full load of lumber, that was big money in those days," said Chuckie O'Brien.

Sylvia's efforts in brokering the new alliance also paid off for Hoffa and the Teamsters. They emerged victorious in the strike, winning increased wages and safety measures for their members and blunting the CIO's offensive. But this was just the beginning. The alliance brokered by Sylvia Pagano would lead to future cooperation that would dwarf the proceeds of a few loads of stolen lumber.

Working for both sides gave the gangsters an education in the myriad ways unions and businesses could be played off each other to make money through fraud, bribes, extortion, and theft. To most Americans, unions were counterweights to big business. To the Mafia, unions *were* big business.

When gangsters controlled unions, they could control entire industries. They could also embezzle funds; extort money in exchange for labor peace; collect bloated salaries; sell sweetheart contracts; create price-fixing cartels; trade election endorsements and campaign contributions for political favors; provide family or friends with no-show jobs; keep competitors out of the market; charge kickbacks for loans…they could even transform a dusty Nevada desert town into an international gambling destination. The American Mafia's prominence in the criminal underworld and society at large is often attributed to Prohibition, which integrated the syndicate into mainstream society and reaped them a massive war chest of financial capital. But it was labor racketeering that added the most diversity to the mob's portfolio and gave them raw power in industry, labor, government, and commerce. At its peak, labor racketeering was part and parcel of the American economy, and Sylvia Pagano was at the center of it.

CHAPTER FIVE

GETTING TIGHT WITH HOFFA

"Hoffa loved Chuck as a true son and Chuck loved Hoffa as a father."

Former IBT President Jackie Presser

By the time Jimmy Hoffa became president of Detroit's IBT Local 299 in 1946, Sylvia and Chuckie were like family.

It raised the eyebrows of those who believed the paternity myth: How could Jimmy Hoffa have the gall to invite his mistress and his illegitimate son into his family home with his wife and two children?

The reality was far less lurid, though still unusual. In Hoffa's sprawling network of close friends and associates, only Sylvia and Chuckie were invited into the nuclear family. Beloved by both Hoffa and his wife, Josephine, Sylvia became indispensable in both of their lives while Chuckie gained a father figure in Mr. Hoffa. "I consider Chuckie one of our family, as do Jo and Barbara and Jim," said Hoffa. "Chuckie was a tot when I met him, the son of a lady who came to Detroit from Kansas City and got a job working for the Teamsters in a potato-chip factory…We raised Chuck from the time he was 6 years-old."

Part of that upbringing was working for the cause: walking picket lines, waving signs, and chanting with his mother and Mr. and Mrs. Hoffa, who had met each other on a picket line in 1936 when Josephine Poszywak was an 18-year-old laundry worker. Sylvia noticed that Chuckie liked to be useful, and she didn't object when Hoffa, with a devilish grin, enlisted Chuckie for special operations like throwing eggs at scabs from a rooftop. Sylvia could only smile when she saw how Chuckie beamed as Hoffa's sidekick.

The IBT represented workers in myriad industries beyond trucking, and their membership included many women.

Even better for Chuckie were summers at the Hoffa's Lake Orion residence, where Sylvia would park Chuckie for weeks at a time while she attended to both union and mob business, including administering Tony Giacalone's bookmaking operation from her Whittier Manor apartment. Sylvia and Hoffa would come and go from the lake house, but "Mama Josephine" took care of Chuckie and showed him how to help with the Hoffa's two young children, Barbara and James Jr. The lake house was where Hoffa began teaching Chuckie practical skills and schooling him in physical fitness. A teetotaler who didn't even drink coffee, Hoffa was known to drop to the floor at any moment and pump out 30 pushups.

On a typical Fourth of July weekend, Sylvia would come in from the city and prepare a family-style Sicilian feast. Hoffa loved her cooking and he valued the companionship she provided to his shy, sickly, and often tipsy wife, who was seeing less of her increasingly important husband.

Chuckie was also seeing less of his mother, whose responsibilities were growing in step with Hoffa's rise. "My mom was always away working, and I was always stuck with somebody," winced Chuckie.

When he wasn't at the lake house, he was often across town at his Uncle Dante's or with his grandparents in Kansas City. Later, he would attend two different military boarding schools. But Sylvia's influence over Chuckie never waned, nor did his loyalty to her. Their love for each other was fortified by their mutual love for the two alpha males whose alliance Sylvia had forged: Jimmy Hoffa and Anthony Giacalone.

Tall, intimidating, and dressed to the nines, "Tony Jack" Giacalone brought Chuckie closer to Sylvia by validating and amplifying her values and teachings. "My mother taught me a lot," said Chuckie. "She taught me about respect for Company [LCN] guys, and loyalty. And she taught me never to give your friends up. She was big on that. On the Sicilian side you're taught, if you see something happen, you don't talk about it. I learned that rule in Kansas City. But I learned it more from Uncle Tony…Uncle Tony, when you met him, you saw a gentleman of stature and respect."

The former strikebreaker was on his way to becoming a made member of an ascendent crime family with enough influence to win itself a seat on the national ruling commission with New York and Chicago. And just as the Family's partnership with Hoffa was making Detroit the center of labor racketeering, Sylvia's old suitor Frank Coppola was making Detroit the center of American narcotics trafficking.

A couple of years after Sylvia introduced Frankie Three Fingers to Jimmy Hoffa, Coppola left Detroit for New Orleans, where KC's Charlie Binaggio was known to visit as Coppola partnered in a slot machine enterprise with Frank Costello, Meyer Lansky, and Sam Carolla, the boss of the Louisiana territory that would soon be run by Carlos Marcello, who would become another close ally of Jimmy Hoffa and a suspect in the Kennedy assassination.

By 1947, Coppola was back in Kansas City and as active as ever when he was arrested by immigration authorities.

After Coppola was deported to Italy in 1948, his politically connected pal, Charlie Binaggio, arranged for the Mexican consul in Kansas City to issue a visa for Coppola to reside in Tijuana as a "student of agriculture and mining." Later, Binaggio did Coppola one better by getting him a temporary visa to return to Kansas City, where Coppola lived at the Pickwick Hotel and socialized with KC and St. Louis gangsters at Bully Rich's Jungle Club on 10th Street, where strippers were backed by jazz musicians. Speaking from Italy decades later, Coppola waxed nostalgic[11] about his time in Kansas City and claimed to have helped swing the 1948 election for his "pal" Harry Truman.

When his visa expired, Coppola moved back to Tijuana where he hosted a visit from Binaggio, Morris "Snag" Klien, and Nick Penna, who had succeeded Charles O'Brien as Binaggio's driver.

At the time, Binaggio represented Coppola's best chance to return to the United States. Like other leading mafiosi, Coppola had invested money in Binaggio's grand plan to elect friendly politicians and open Missouri to police protected gambling and vice.

A year later, Coppola hosted a summit in Tijuana attended by several Sicilian gangsters and some Americans including KC's Geatano Lococo (whose daughter was married to Sylvia's cousin, Phil Scaglia); Tony Lopiparo from St. Louis; Sam Carolla from New Orleans; Frank Bompensiero of San Diego; and Sebastian Gallo from Detroit. American

---

[11] "I started life as a peasant. When I left the big town Kansas City and beautiful America, I came back to the farm. At night I dream I'm back in Kansas City with pals—Tom Pendergast and Harry Truman. People didn't like Harry's guts, and when Harry made important political trips, he'd call me and say, 'Frankie, you and your boys get your ass to these places and soften up those goddamn sons of bitches.' How many times we drank the best bourbon in the Muehlbach Hotel!"

investigators believed the summit concerned border smuggling but also suspected that it sanctioned the hit on the man who had arranged for Coppola to live in the very place the death sentence was decreed—the man Sylvia's son claimed as his godfather. And while Chuckie's claim to Binaggio appears accurate, Vincent Piersante, the Deputy Chief of Detectives for the Detroit Police Department, believed that Sylvia's boyfriend, Frank Coppola, was Chuckie's godfather.

Charlie Binaggio's funeral at the Holy Rosary Church, where Sylvia was baptized in KC's Little Italy.

After Charlie Binaggio and Charlie Gargotta were killed in the double murder at the Democratic club, Coppola left Mexico for Italy, where his connections in the U.S. earned him a seat with the also-deported Lucky Luciano and other top Sicilian mafiosi on the ruling commission of the syndicate's international narcotics network. Nicola Gentile wrote that in 1957, he and Coppola and Luciano attended a banquet in the Grand Hotel et des Palmes in Palermo that decided the fate of New York don Albert Anastasia, who was famously murdered in a Manhattan barber's chair later that month. One of the few Americans present at the summit was Giovanni "Papa John" Priziola, whose attendance marked Detroit's high status in the international syndicate.

Working with Luciano and other top Sicilians, Sylvia's former sweetheart helped establish global connections and smuggling routes that dominated the heroin trade for decades and included the "French Connection" of Hollywood fame. Lost in most accounts of the heroin trade is the key role Detroit played through Coppola's recipients in the Motor City: Papa John Priziola and Raffaele "Jimmy Q" Quasarano, both of whom hailed from Coppola's hometown of Partinico, Sicily.

"Detroit was the primary point of drug imports," said Bureau of Narcotics agent Charles Siragusa. "And the Detroit Mob fed the rest of the country, even New York."

Moving heroin from Detroit was complicated, but less so than it might have been in other cities. Detroit's relationship with Hoffa and the Teamsters allowed Priziola and Quasarano to exploit trucking in ways that distributed their product efficiently and minimized their exposure. "Hoffa was not at all averse to using the Teamsters Union as a means of protection for those who were associated with the narcotics traffic," said Detective Piersante. "By protection I mean he went as far as giving some of those involved jobs with the union."

That included Priziola and Quasarano, who were employed as business agents for Local 985. Known as the "jukebox local," Local 985 had been chartered by Jimmy Hoffa and Bert Brennan as part of a plan for the mob to monopolize jukeboxes and exploit other elements of Detroit's burgeoning music business. Hoffa and Brennan put their wives on the Local 985 payroll under their maiden names for no-show jobs and handed the presidency to Sylvia's friend, William "Bill" Bufalino, who had a unique set of credentials that distinguished him from his peers and gave him unique status in the underworld. Like Tony Provenzano in New Jersey and Babe Triscaro in Cleveland, Bill Bufalino was both a made man in the Mafia and a ranking Teamsters official. But Bufalino was also a highly regarded defense attorney whose clients included Jimmy Hoffa. Bufalino also benefited from familial currency: his wife, Marie Antoinette, was the daughter of Detroit Family elder Frank Meli, and his first cousin was Pennsylvania's Russell Bufalino, who was arguably the most influential Mafia boss in the United States and one of Jimmy Hoffa's key allies.

Sylvia's friend and associate, Bill Bufalino

Sylvia could never have predicted the myriad implications of introducing Hoffa and the Detroit Teamsters to the Mafia. She had benefited from each organization, and self-interest would naturally have motivated her to help form an alliance. And pay off for Sylvia it did. As the 1940's closed, Chuckie O'Brien's mother had steady work as a union secretary and a valuable niche as a liaison between organized labor and organized crime. Jimmy Hoffa and Tony Giacalone became close friends, but both men trusted Sylvia more than they did each other, and for the next quarter century, most of their communication was done through *Facci*.

CHAPTER 6

DIRTY LAUNDRY

"Dalitz met Hoffa through Sylvia Pagano, who introduced the rising Teamsters official to the Detroit underworld."

Investigative Journalist James Neff, 1988

In 1950, Sylvia was 33 years-old and living in an apartment at 4570 North Lawn Street in Detroit. Her son, Chuckie, age 16, was also listed at the address but was mostly away at military school. Sylvia worked as a secretary for Local 876 of the Retail Clerks Union, whose office was in the Detroit Teamsters building, and whose members paid dues to the Teamsters. "The Retail Clerks and the Meat Cutters could not win a strike without the Teamsters Union," said Jimmy Hoffa. "And as long as I sat in the negotiations, the employers were on alert that if they had a fight with the retail clerks, they were going to have a fight with the Teamsters Union." Robert Kennedy later wrote that Hoffa had "literally stolen" Local 876 and presided over "wide-scale misuse of the local's funds" while Sylvia served as local secretary.

The Retail Clerks was not the only union that Hoffa relied on Sylvia to help bring under Teamsters command. The union with the closest ties to Hoffa's Detroit Teamsters was the International Laundry Workers Union. And just as she had found herself bringing Hoffa and the Detroit LCN together, Sylvia was now similarly positioned between Hoffa and John Paris, who was both the head of Local 129 of the Laundry Workers Union and Sylvia's new husband.

Paris was a full-blooded Italian whose original surname was Parisi. He was born two years before Sylvia in Ontario, Canada, where he grew up with a sister who later married Hollywood actor Edward Arnold. In one of his more credible claims, a notorious Hoffa soldier named Joe Franco said that he introduced Sylvia to John. Paris was a fixture in the Detroit labor scene, acting as an AFL representative in strikes involving a variety of unions and serving as secretary-treasurer for the Detroit and Wayne County Federation of Labor even as he held the presidency of Local 129 of the Laundry Workers Union. Sylvia and her new husband lived in Bloomfield Township in a house on top of a hill surrounded with a moat and illuminated with floodlights. Two white German Shepards patrolled the premises.

Circled: Sylvia's second husband, John Paris

In 1950, the Teamsters and Laundry Workers were both negotiating contracts with the Detroit Institute of Laundry, an owners' association led by Moe Dalitz, a laundry tycoon and leading member of Detroit's Jewish Purple Gang. Sylvia was positioned to represent the interests of both unions by communicating between her husband and Hoffa and consulting with and advising both on strategy and planning. She spoke with authority earned from her in-the-trenches experience as an organizer and her close association with the Teamsters, the Retail Clerks, and the Laundry Workers. With Sylvia working behind the scenes, the International Laundry Workers Union would later merge into the IBT, but in 1950, each union was negotiating separate contracts with the laundry owners. Fortunatley for both Hoffa and John Paris, Sylvia had the ear of Moe Dalitz.

The timelines and circumstances of Jimmy Hoffa's introduction to Moe Dalitz vary widely in different tellings, but most accounts put Sylvia at the center of their affiliation. Dalitz and his Purple Gang preceded the Detroit LCN in the labor rackets, and they had alternately clashed and cooperated with the Teamsters during the 1930's labor wars. As the Italians slowly out-competed the Jews in Detroit's rackets, Dalitz expanded into Cleveland, where he established a union-protected laundry cartel and became a leader in the group of Jewish racketeers known as the "Kosher Nostra," which would later work closely with the Teamsters and the Mafia to make Moe Dalitz the "Godfather of Las Vegas."

Sylvia's admirer Moe Dalitz in his later years as the "Godfather of Las Vegas."

Dalitz biographer Michael Newton described Sylvia as a "former Dalitz paramour." Hoffa biographer Aurthur Sloane said that Dalitz, like other powerful men in labor and crime, simply "had a thing" for Sylvia. Regardless, Sylvia appears to have known Dalitz before she married the boss of the union that represented Dalitz's workers, and evidence points to her as the facilitator of a $16,000 bribe the Dalitz-controlled Detroit Laundry Institute paid to her husband, John Paris, to settle the Laundry Worker's contract.

Meanwhile, the laundry owner's negotiations with the Teamsters dragged on. The owners had run up against Isaac Litwak, the president of Local 285 who was stubborn in his demands for a five-day work week. The impasse was evolving into violence, and Litwak threatened a strike. In the machinations that followed, Sylvia quelled the rough stuff, prevented the strike, and brokered another historically significant alliance by bringing Jimmy Hoffa and Moe Dalitz together to break the deadlock between the laundry owners and the Teamsters.

"They said I knew Moe Dalitz and that he was a big deal in the Mafia," Hoffa later said. "Hell yes, I knew Dalitz. I've known him since way back when he owned a string of laundries in Detroit and we threatened him with a strike. Those were the laundries Ike Litwak was organizing and where they kept beating the hell out of him. We finally got our contract."

Hoffa didn't mention what various witnesses later testified to: that the contract was promptly signed on the owners' terms after Dalitz met with Hoffa and paid him $17,000[12] in cash. The members of Local 285 would have to wait for their five-day work week. Dalitz, though, got more than a sweetheart contract out of the deal. With the help of men like John Paris and Jimmy Hoffa, he used the Laundry Workers Union to force his competitors to fix prices and pay

---

[12] Approximately $230,000 in 2026 dollars

dues to his owners' association. Stability and higher profits resulted for most of the companies, and few complained.

How much Sylvia profited from such transactions is unknown, but bringing Jimmy Hoffa and Moe Dalitz together marked another diplomatic coup for *Facci*—one that would impact American history by shaping the development and direction of the city of Las Vegas.

CHAPTER SEVEN

HOFFA GOES NATIONAL

"Working by themselves, such racketeers as John Dioguardi and Anthony Corallo present a dangerous enough problem, but when they have the backing of top officers in the nations largest union, particualarly James R. Hoffa…the situation becomes one for national alarm."

Senator John McClellan

By connecting Hoffa to the Detroit *Borgata* and Moe Dalitz, Sylvia had set Hoffa up for national recognition among the crime families. Dalitz's Cleveland connections included Bill Presser and Louis "Babe" Triscaro, who would become close Hoffa allies in the key union stronghold of Ohio. In Chicago, Sylvia and Dalitz connected Hoffa to Paul "Red" Dorfman, a native Detroiter Dalitz knew from his days in the Purple Gang and who now ran Chicago's waste handler's union. Hoffa became close to Red and his stepson, Allen Dorfman, whom Hoffa set up in the insurance business with an extremely lucrative monopoly on Teamsters health insurance plans. Sylvia acted as a liason between Hoffa and Allen Dorfman and became very close to Dorfman both socially and professionaly. Close associations with other key Chicago Outfit leaders and union officials fell into place for Hoffa, and he soon had the support of enough union delegates to dominate the IBT in the Midwest.

But Hoffa's ambitions weren't limited to middle America. Hoffa needed the support of the East Coast underworld to realize his dream of becoming International IBT President. Here again, Sylvia made the connection: "With Sylvia's help, Hoffa arranged a meeting in a New York hotel, probably in 1954, with LCN members who controlled unions," wrote Jack Goldsmith.

Sylvia's main connection in the East was Anthony "Tony Pro" Provenzano, a former truck driver whose cousin was married to Tony Giacalone in Detroit. One of Hoffa's lawyers, Frank Ragano, described Tony Pro as, "a swaggering, broad-shouldered man with a street brawler's vocabulary and a penchant for glittering silk suits and pinky rings." Chuckie remembered meeting Provenzano when he was a young boy in Detroit and calling him "Uncle Tony" for the rest of his life. Sylvia often socialized with Tony Pro on their many trips to Miami, where Tony Pro, Jimmy Hoffa, and Tony Giacalone all had apartments that were available to Sylvia. Like Bill Bufalino in Detroit and Babe Triscaro in Cleveland, Tony Pro was both a made member of the Mafia and a high-ranking Teamsters official. As boss of the largest IBT local in New Jersey, Tony Pro was vital to Hoffa's ambitions.

In addition to Tony Pro, the meeting that Sylvia arranged included Mathew "Matty the Horse" Ianniello, Anthony "Tony Ducks" Corallo, and John "Johnny Dio" Dioguardi, a power in the Amalgamated Meat Cutter's Union whose viciousness knew no bounds and whose collaboration with Hoffa offers an example of how the Mafia and the Teamsters used each other to mutual benefit.

Hoffa's path to presidential victory depended on control of the joint council of New York's IBT locals. If Hoffa could install a loyal ally as joint council president, he could count on their large bloc of votes when he ran for IBT President. His chosen candidate was John O'Rourke, a veteran of Eddie McGrath's Hell's Kitchen gang of Irish waterfront racketeers who carried the scars of several bullet wounds.

Johnny Dio and Hoffa worked out a deal wherby Hoffa gave Dio official union charters for seven "paper" or "phantom" IBT locals. The locals had no real members, but in joint council elections, every local was represented evenly, regardless of size. The seven paper locals swung the election to O'Rourke and Hoffa had his path to victory while Dio and his mob associates had seven new locals and all the labor rackteering opportunites that went with them. Dio's wife later became close to Hoffa's wife and by extension, to Sylvia, who was Josephine Hoffa's closest friend.

Johnny Dio

Hoffa's relationship with Dio came under national scrutiny after an incident which illustrates the type of man Dio was and Hoffa's lack of scruples in associating with. In New York City on April 5, 1956, crusading labor journalist Victor Riesel hosted rebel Teamsters on his radio show to discuss corruption and reform. Later that evening, as Riesel was exiting Lindy's Restaraunt, a subordinate of Dio's threw acid into Riesel's eyes, permanently blinding him. After Riesels's assailant was found dead and other witnesses refused to testify, the charges against Johnny Dio were dismissed.

Victor Riesel

Sylvia had connected Hoffa to crime families in Detroit, Cleveland, Chicago, and the Northeast. Now her old friends in Kansas City wanted in on the action.

CHAPTER EIGHT

WORK STOPPAGE

"It is apparent that the jurisdictional demands of Kansas City's Teamsters brought the building and construction industry in that area to a complete halt…it depressed one of the nation's great metropolitan centers, and cowed what was one of its most vigorous industries…This committee and the Congress should look with deep concern at this sordid account of free men, afraid to work, terrorized by the gangster tactics of those to whom the Congress itself has given privilege and authority."

U.S. House Special Subcommittee on Strikes and Racketeering, June, 1953.

While Hoffa was rising to national prominence, Sylvia sent Chuckie back to Kansas City in 1950 to live with his grandparents on Independence Avenue and attend Cardinal Glennon High School. The old neighborhood hadn't changed much; still mostly Italian and still under the strong influence of men like Joe Filardo, the owner of the Roma Bakery, who Chuckie came to revere as the epitome of an old school "man of honor." Chuckie also idolized his uncle and next-door neighbor, Mariano Scaglia, who embodied the ways of a traditional mafioso and remained well-respected in spite of his demotion for avenging his brother's murder in Pueblo decades earlier. At Cardinal Glennon, Chuckie was a good athlete who lettered in varsity basketball and football, but he seemed less interested in sports than in following in the footsteps of his hero and surrogate father back in Detroit.

The first step was becoming a truck driver. According to Chuckie, "Uncle Nick and Uncle Cork" set him up with his first job. The Civella brothers certainly wouldn't have balked at doing Chuckie—and Sylvia—a favor. Nick Civella was poised to become a power in labor racketeering, and connections to Detroit would be essential. In the meantime, other non-Italian racketeers—"peckerwoods," as Civella called them—had already made the KC Teamsters a prime example of the corruption and violence that would characterize the union under Hoffa's reign.

When Chuckie proudly joined IBT Local 541, he couldn't wait to tell Hoffa. Sylvia, too, would be pleased, and Chuckie longed for anything that would bring him closer to the mother he was so often separated from. In this regard, a young lady named Maryann Giaramita was a pyschologicaly unsurprising attraction for Chuckie. She grew up in the same neighborhood as Sylvia and bore a physical resemblance to *Facci*. Maryann's mother—like Sylvia's—worked as a seamstress in a KC clothing factory. Maryann even attended Sylvia's old school, Manual High. Chuckie fell hard for Maryann, and the young couple would soon return to Detroit as man and wife.

Sylvia's daughter-in-law, Maryanne Giaramita, in the Manual High yearbook.

In the meantime, teenaged Chuckie was far removed from union power and politics, but he joined KC Local 541 at a time when it was becoming embroiled in events that shocked citizens who were hardly strangers to crime and corruption. Local 541 in the early 1950's offers a case study in labor racketeering and serves as a window into the world that Sylvia's son was preparing to enter.

When Chuckie joined Local 541, its president was a gun-toting peckerwood named Orville Ring, who had his sights set on controlling all the IBT locals in the region and the political spoils they represented. "If you control the joint council, you are a power in city elections," said Ring. "You can pass the word along through the business agents to some 30,000 families."

Mr. Ring, who wore heavy, skull-cracking rings on both hands, built a power base of hand-picked business agents with criminal and prizefighting backgrounds. He was able to deputize many of these men through his political connections to Jackson County Sheriff J.A. Purdome, a machine politician from the Rabbit faction of the Democratic Party who had been reelected in the 1948 election with the backing of Sylvia's former beau Frank Coppola and her son's godfather, Charlie Binaggio.

In the lead-up to the joint council election, Ring's henchmen stayed busy coercing votes and shutting down opposition. "A campaign of terrorism and intimidation was going on for a month before the election," said union dissident Edward Chevlin. "Everybody was being muscled in the halls. The agents of 541 were walking around with deputy sheriffs' badges and guns. Goons were all over the place, and you could look out of the window almost any day and see somebody laying there with his head cut open."

Chevlin would soon find himself with his own head cut open. As an honest Teamsters official and reformer who had protested against treasury looting and other skullduggery, he was a marked man. When Chevlin confronted Ring at the union hall on Linwood Boulevard, Ring punched him to the floor. "Ring wears a big ring as brass knuckles, and he slugged me," said Chevlin. "Two business agents stood by, one with a gun. Ring cut open my head. Then he started choking me. I thought I was going to die."

The Kansas City area IBT headquarters was at 116 West Linwood Boulevard until moving to its current location at 4501 Emanuel Cleaver II Boulevard in 1967. In the 1930's and 40's, the "Teamsters Democratic Club" shared the building with the Rabbit faction of KC's Democratic Party machine. The basement was used for shooting dice.

Nobody expected Chevlin to return to the union hall, but return he did. "Every morning, I didn't know whether I would be beat up or killed," he said. Things only got worse when Chevlin rallied opposition to Ring's candidacy, Chevlin appealed to the sheriff's office and the KCPD for a license to carry a gun, but was refused. He got one anyway and brandished it to get through a gauntlet of brick-fisted business agents who were laying for him after a meeting of the rank-and-file. Police later siezed Chevlin's gun and tickited him with a fine. Shortly thereafter, an unidentified assaliant attacked Chevlin in the union hall parking lot, breaking his dentures and leaving him bleeding and half-concious on the pavement. When he still refused to back down, his wife began receiving threatening phone calls: "Ed is lying dead in an alley; come and get him…"

Orville Ring lost the election but was able to muscle the rightful winner from power and become President of Joint Council 56. But Ring wasn't satisfied with control over the regional Teamsters; he wanted control over numerous other unions that were represented by the American Federation of Labor. Even as the drama with Edward Chevlin was playing out, Ring was fomenting a series of inter-union labor disputes that crippled Kansas City and gave the U.S. government an alarming example of how the Teamsters held the power to paralyze the nation.

If going to war with other unions was conterproductive to the cause and unbecoming of a labor leader, men like Orville Ring didn't care. "Teamster locals can dominate other AFL unions," Ring told a reporter. "If they don't go along, the Teamsters shut down their jobs by refusing to haul any supplies."

And that's exactly what Ring did. Beginning in 1952—the year Sylvia's son joined his local—Ring began a series of jurisdictional disputes with other unions that effectively halted construction in Kansas City. When supply refusals weren't enough to shut down a jobsite, Ring employed violence, intimidation, and sabatogue. Unions representing plumbers, carpenters, electricians, laborers and others were all brought to their knees by the economic power and gangster tactics of the KC Teamsters. 22,500 Kansas Citians were out of work, and the stoppages jolted Washinton D.C. Four major military defense projects were centered in the Kansas City area, and each of them suffered stoppages that hampered the military's production of munitions and other hardware during the Korean War. A two-month stoppage at the Claycomo jet-wing plant resulted from, "a dispute over which union had the right to push a button to start an automatic heating apparatus on which the comfort of the workers themselves depended."

Congress stepped in in 1953 by authorizing a subcommitee investigation led by Represetative Clare Hoffman of Michigan. Hoffman's subcommittee was already hearing testimony in Detroit, where it was investigating Jimmy Hoffa and Bill Bufalino's activities in the jukebox local. What the subcommitte found in Kansas City was, "one of the most forbidding chapters in the history of American unions."

The subcommittee's report painted a vivid picture:

"…the fear, the unconscionably vicious assaults, the need for bodyguards, the brazen evidence of kidnaping, the promiscuous granting of deputy sheriff commissions, the widespread practice of carrying deadly weapons, the roving gangs patrolling construction job sites, and the strong-armed convoys in high-powered cars, including Mr. Ring's air-conditioned Cadillac. Broken teeth, a maimed arm, or a crippled shoulder were typical of the victims' lot. Many unions see a threat to their continued existence in this obvious Teamster bid for power and control. With some of the groups having literally reached the armed-camp stage, effective steps must be taken promptly to prevent the violence from spreading."

Orville Ring at his Missouri farm with his wife, Rose, and his air-conditioned Cadillac

While Orville Ring's Local 541 figured most prominently in the hearings, other KC Teamsters were also scrutinized, including Local 955 President Lee Quisenberry, a 250 pound bruiser who had survived three shootings between 1947-1950 that were thought to have been ordered by the KC Crime Family. The committee heard testimony from a federal meat inspector who said that assailants entered his home and beat his wife because he refused to knuckle under to Quisenberry's demands during a power struggle with the CIO at the Rice Sausage Company. Two other witnesses testified that Quisenberry and three other union men kidnapped, intimidated, and assaulted them in the midst of a dispute with the Mauer-Neuer Meatpacking Company.

Edward Chevlin took the stand and described his beatings at the hands of Orville Ring and other Local 541 officials. Burried within Chevlin's testimony is an anecdote about Jimmy Hoffa that seems to have escaped publication in the voluminous accounts of Hoffa's life. Chevlin testified that back in 1940, he went to Detroit as an organizer with the CIO, which was feuding with the Teamsters until a year later when Sylvia's alliance helped Hoffa repel the CIO's offensive during the lumber strike. Chevlin said that he was organizing for the CIO outside an optical manufacturing company when he was accosted by four men. "I got a majority of the membership signed up, and one morning I came out of the Keller Hotel and there were four men in a car, and these four men…I was told, and I later identified a picture, that Jimmy Hoffa was one of them, and they beat me up with chains."

Chevlin knew that the same subcommittee was investigating Hoffa and the jukebox local in Detroit and he seems to have have been reluctant to bring too much heat on the rising labor leader; Chevlin hedged his statement: "…at that time he was young and misguided, probably misled by some of the older people in the union, and I don't think that, at least I don't know it to be a fact, that Hoffa would use those methods again today…I think he is a pretty smart boy myself."

The subcommittee probably agreed that Hoffa was a smart fellow after Representative Wint Smith of Kansas took over from Hoffman as committee chair. Hoffa immediately hired former Kansas governor Payne Ratner as one of his attorneys. A short time later, the hearings in Detroit and Kansas City were cancelled and nobody was indicted. "Newspaper men were astounded," Robert Kennedy later wrote. "Could Jimmy Hoffa's pressure reach into the halls of the legislative branch of the Government? They went to Chairman Smith and asked why his committee had closed up shop. 'The pressure comes from way up there and I just can't talk about it any more specifically than that,' was the answer."

As KC's labor strife raged on, Orville Ring met in St. Louis with Hoffa's Cleveland associate Louis "Babe" Triscaro. A week later, Jimmy Hoffa himself arrived in Kansas City and helped resolve the conflict. Kansas City breathed a sigh of relief as its ten-week-long labor war subsided and construction and commerce resumed.

Following the subcommittee's dissolution, a Jackson County grand jury indicted Orville Ring and seven others. Most of the cases were dismised by judges or dropped by prosecutors. Honest Edward Chevlin wasn't so lucky. County prosecutor Richard Phelps revived Chevlin's earlier gun violation and charged him with assualt with intent to kill. When the jury deadlocked in favor of aquittal, Phelps charged him again for felonious assault. After another hung jury, Phelps broke precedent and charged Chevlin a *third* time, finally winning a conviction after violating discovery by withholding

Chevlin's "missing" hospital records. Phelps later won a second term as prosecuter after being endorsed by Kansas City's Labor League for Political Education. "Following extensive indictments, only jail term goes to foe of union leaders," marveled the Kansas City Star.

Watching and learning in the wings of KC's 1953 labor war were Nick Civella and his crime family—crouched and ready to pounch amdist the chaos. When Orville Ring resigned from the union on March 1, 1954, many assumed he had done so under pressure from the IBT, but Orville Ring was actually an early causulty in the Mafia's takeover of the KC Teamsters. It wasn't an outright purge of the peckerwoods—Nick Civella would make key allies out of some of them—but a new era was dawning, and the Italians were ascendant.

After threatening Orville Ring into early retirement on his farm, Civella rigged the election and installed a loyalist named Ernie Anderson as interim president of Local 541. As the elction approached, Anderson was challenged by a Teamster named Emmett Eslinger. On April 26, 1954, Eslinger's wife found his car parked along Highway 71. In the car she found her husband dead with his head bashed in and his throat slashed.

That same year, close Civella associate Sam Ancona took over Local 955 from Lee Quisenberry. Ancona would also become Secretary-Treasurer of Joint Council 56. John Balestrere found work as a business agent for Local 955, and Tripoli Milone was appointed Secretary-Treasurer of Local 541. Local 41, which had escaped scrutiny in the congressional investigation, became the domain of Civella's most valuable ally, Roy Lee Williams.

Jimmy Hoffa (sitting) with KC's Roy Williams and an unidentified woman standing behind. Hoffa always wore white socks, a fashion faux pas that exasperated the sartorial sensibilities of his Mafia associates.

Missouri Teamster Photograph Collection, (S0599) The State Historical Society of Missouri

One of 12 children from a poor farming family, Roy Williams had been a working-stiff truck driver for a decade before shipping off to Europe in World War II, where his valor earned him 5 bronze stars and a silver star. The returning hero got a job with the Teamsters after the war and became a successful organizer. Williams and Nick Civella became friends while they were both serving on a Democratic Party committee that fielded candidates in Jackson County. Civella did favors for Williams and expected favors in return. Williams would later discover just how serious Civella's expectations were.

Jimmy Hoffa made another trip to Kansas City to personally preside over Williams' election and meet with Nick Civella. According to Williams, Hoffa met frequently with Civella in Kansas City and Chicago. In her role as Hoffa's main emisarry to LCN, it's likely that Sylvia arranged some of these meetings. Regardless, Sylvia became a natural and efficient intermediary between Hoffa and her old friend—her son's "Uncle Nick"—in her hometown of Kansas City.

CHAPTER NINE

HOFFA VERSUS KENNEDY

"There is not a gangster in the U.S. that does not have a link with Hoffa and the four or five top men around him."

Robert F. Kennedy

"But to hear Kennedy when he was grandstanding in front of the McClellan Committee you might have thought I was making as much out of the pension fund as the Kennedys made out of selling [illegal] whiskey."

Jimmy Hoffa

Sylvia's son returned to Detroit a married man at age 19. Chuckie and Maryann would soon have two children: son and namesake Charles, and daughter Josephine, whom Chuckie and Maryann named after Josephine Hoffa. Baby Charles's godfather was Chuckie's best friend from Kansas City, Joe Mike Cristifano. Josphine's godfather was Vince Meli, a World War II hero, Notre Dame graduate, music industry entrepernuer, and influential Detroit Family *capo* who was both the son-in-law of Santo Perrone and the brother of Bill Bufalino's wife. Meli would later become a suspect in the disappearance and murder of Jimmy Hoffa.

Sylvia's granddaughter's godfather, Vince Meli, typified Detroit's second generation mafiosi: college-educated but streetwise, diversified in business, and tightly married within the Family.

The Jimmy Hoffa Chuckie returned to was, at age 39, the youngest International Vice President in IBT history and a nationally recognized leader in American labor. Weekends at the lake house resumed, and Chuckie began beseeching Hoffa for a job.

Chuckie was also getting reaquainted with Uncle Tony Jack. Anthony Giacalone was now a fully-fledged member of the Detroit Family and an ever more important link, through Sylvia, to the second-most powerful Teamster in the nation. Giacalone saw Sylvia as indispensable in his relationship to his most valuable asset, not only as a liason, but someone who could reason with Hoffa and sway his decisions. "Sylvia is the only person around this country that can handle Jimmy Hoffa," an admiring Giacalone later said on tape. Like Moe Dalitz, Tony Jack also "had a thing" for Sylvia.

No wonder, then, that Giacalone happily did favors for *Facci*. In about 1954, Uncle Tony invited Sylvia's son to the Grecain Gardens restaurant and led him to a private room where Family boss Joe Zerilli sat around a table with other made men. "Tell them what you told me," said Giaclaone.

Chuckie took a deep breath and responded, "On my honor I will never betray any relationship I have with all of you."

The men rose, hugged and kissed Chuckie, and invited him to sit down and break bread with them. "The entire event was a favor to Sylvia," wrote Chuckie's stepson, "whom the top guys adored and who wanted to fortify her son's Sicilian connections and identity…Chuckie took his Kansas City heritage, his mother's values, and his teenage pledge to Uncle Tony more seriously than any other obligation in his life."

Around the same time, Chuckie shared another, less ritualistic rite of passage with Mr. Hoffa, who invited Chuckie into his office and asked him, "Why do you think you could make a pimple on a business agent's ass?"

Chuckie walked out of the office as an official organizer for Local 299. His real job, though, was doing whatever the Old Man required. Bodyguard, babysitter, strongarm, gofer, go-between…Chuckie did all these things, and never complained. "Mr. Hoffa knew I would never say no to him," said Chuckie. "A lot of people would run away because they didn't want to get involved. He knew he could count on me."

But Chuckie was hardly the only one to get involved. The term, "Hoffa's right hand man," has been applied to Bert Brennan, Rolland McMaster, Frank Sheeran, Joe Franco, Barney Baker, and assorted other Teamster-affiliated tough guys whose loyalty Hoffa could count on. Like the increasing number of Mafia dons he associated with, Jimmy Hoffa surrounded himself with an insulating army of intimidating soldiers. But only Chuckie was family, and his duties included working with Sylvia to look after Hoffa's wife and children.

In 1955, Hoffa began negotiating pension plans for Teamsters in 22 states. The Central States Pension Fund brought in $10 million in its first year and would soon swell into the billions. It was a monumental achievement, but one ripe for exploitation. "The Fund became a special bank where loans depended almost entierly on the the right kickbacks or the right organized crime connections," wrote investigative journalist Stephen Brill.

The Fund was cause for celebration among Teamsters rank-and-file, but it drew scrutiny from investigators, and pension fraud was added to the long list of accusations that Robert Kennedy was preparing to level at Jimmy Hoffa and other leading union officials and gangsters on live television.

Kennedy was serving as chief counsel for the United States Senate Select Committee on Improper Activities in Labor and Management, also known as the McClellan Committee. The hearings spanned a two-year period and made Jimmy Hoffa a household name. Sylvia and Chuckie's names came up in the proceedings:

Mr. Kennedy: He [John Paris] was married to a woman by the name of Sylvia?

Mr. Hoffa: Yes, sir.

Mr. Kennedy: She is a friend of you and your family?

Mr. Hoffa: That is right.

Mr. Kennedy: And they have a son?

Mr. Hoffa: That is right.

Mr. Kennedy: What is his name?

Mr. Hoffa: Charles O'Brien.

Mr. Kennedy: And he is with your union, is he?

Mr. Hoffa: That is right.

Kennedy went on to grill Hoffa about Sylvia's workplace at Local 876 of the Retail Clerk's Union, which Kennedy accused Hoffa of pilfering. Chuckie had joined his mother on the payroll of the Hoffa-dominated local, but the Committee had discovered that Chuckie had spent the entire summer of 1956 doing remodeling work on the Hoffa lake house while collecting his union salary.

Mr. Kennedy: Mr. O'Brien was a paid employee of the retail clerks?

Mr. Bellino: Mr. O'Brien was a paid employee of the retail clerks for the whole year of 1956.

Mr. Kennedy: But during that particular period of time, according to the testimony of the previous witness, he was up doing some work on Mr. Hoffa's private property?

Mr. Bellino: Yes, sir.

On March 14, 1957, Hoffa was arrested for planting a spy into the McClellan Committee and paying him for inside information. Hoffa denied the charges and was later acquitted, but the trial represented the new normal for Hoffa. He would spend the next six years surrounded by lawyers as he fought what he called a "blood feud" with Robert Kennedy.

The hearings did hold a silver lining for Hoffa. IBT President Dave Beck, Hoffa's only superior, was indicted by the Committee and forced to step down. This development paved the way for Hoffa's presidency, and with the help of Roy Williams and a united bloc of delegates from Kansas City, Jimmy Hoffa became International IBT President on October 4, 1957, with 72 percent of the vote. Robert Kennedy claimed the election was, "rigged from start to finish," but Hoffa's popularity with the rank-and-file was indisputable, and it would only grow.

Left to right: Sylvia, Josephine Hoffa, Sylvia's grandson, Chuckie O'Brien, and Jimmy Hoffa sit at the head of a dozen-seat table in Miami Beach, celebrating Hoffa's election to IBT President.

Hoffa's victory required him to spend more time at IBT headquarters in Washington D.C. and less time with his wife and two teenage children. Here again, Sylvia became indispensable to Hoffa. Her husband, John Paris, had died earlier that same year at age 44 while visiting his sister in Burbank, California. With no husband to look after, Sylvia was able to shift attention onto Hoffa's family. But Sylvia could only do so much, and her son was also needed. When Hoffa asked Chuckie to move his own family into the Hoffa's Detroit residence with Josephine and the kids, Chuckie dutifully obliged.

It was a tight fit, but Chuckie's good-natured attitude, his wife's willingness, and Sylvia's grit helped make it work. Chuckie's wife and Hoffa's daughter were close in age and became best friends. Chuckie's son and namesake described the homes he lived in from first through eighth grade: "The house on Robson Street was a nice older two-story brick home with a small yard and a finished basement. There was a milk chute on the side of the house and sometimes when we got locked out, I would crawl through it. When Uncle Jimmy was there, he would mow the lawn and rake leaves. Uncle Jimmy was the closest thing I had to a grandfather. He taught me how to shoot a rifle and what to look for when hunting deer. He was a health fanatic. At the lake house, they had a four-car garage where Uncle Jimmy had a gym with weights and stuff. The walk from the house to the garage was about the length of a football field and he would pick up two big cement blocks in each hand and every time he walked to and from the garage he'd carry those heavy blocks. He was *strong*.

"Shop stewards—guys who were just regular truck drivers and other working guys—would come to the house to talk to Uncle Jimmy. He treated them with a lot of respect and care."

This was a sentiment that even Hoffa's critics agreed with, "He was accessible to members and had a computer-like memory for their names and their particular personal problems," said investigative reporter Jonathan Kwitny. "He was, in short, always a crook, but always a Teamster."

Hoffa biographer Arthur Sloane wrote that Hoffa's children viewed Chuckie as a "fun-loving and personable surrogate older brother who was never too busy to take their mother to the doctor or do an endless variety of other errands."

Unfortunately for Josephine Hoffa, doctor appointments were all too frequent as her fragile health was undermined by her worsening alcoholism. "This woman belongs in an institution," Tony Giacalone told Chuckie's wife, Maryann. "I think that Jimmy is hurting this woman more by not putting her in a hospital where she can get the proper care." Giacalone's concern for Josephine Hoffa seemed sincere, but Tony Jack would later exploit Josephine's addiction for personal gain.

CHAPTER TEN

THE FUND

"[The Teamsters Union] is indeed, a racket—perhaps the world's biggest, a bigger money-maker for the mob than all the betting in Las Vegas. In fact, without the Teamsters there might not even be a Las Vegas, at least as we know it."

Investigative Journalist Jonathan Kwitny, 1979.

With Hoffa calling the shots and hand-picking the trustees, the Teamsters Central States Pension Fund was becoming "the Mafia's bank." Borrowers who were shunned by conventional banks could, with the right connections, borrow large sums of money at favorable interest rates so long as they paid kickbacks to Hoffa and other Teamsters and mafiosi who arranged the loans. "The lion's share of fund loans involved a cash kickback, a mob connection, friendship, or all three," wrote retired FBI agent William Ouseley.

Sylvia's friend Moe Dalitz was an early beneficiary of the Fund, and the first of many to invest the money in Las Vegas resorts and casinos. Dalitz set up a formula in which frontmen worked through mobsters to obtain loans, pay kickbacks to both their LCN sponsors and Hoffa, and bring their sponsors in as silent partners. The mobsters would then get choice concessions inside the resorts and jobs aplenty for their associates. The biggest prize though, was the skim: millions of tax-free dollars stolen from casino counting rooms and couriered to crime bosses around the country. According to Chuckie O'Brien, Hoffa had a piece of the skim from as many as eight Las Vegas casinos.

By the early 1960's most of the major casinos in Las Vegas were Teamster-financed and Mafia-controlled. Moe Dalitz had managed to polish his image and endear himself to civic leaders and politicians, in part by building the Teamsters-financed Sunrise Hospital and Las Vegas Convention Center. Dalitz fit in well with polite company and he became a well-respected philanthropist, even earning "Man of the Year" awards from the American Cancer Research Center and the Anti-Defamation League.

But Sylvia's pal was known as the "Godfather of Las Vegas" for other reasons. Future IBT President Jackie Presser told the FBI, "The individual who oversees the operations for the LCN families in Las Vegas is Moe Dalitz. Dalitz makes certain that there is no cheating with regard to the skim money taken out of the casinos and further, that there is no fighting among families for control of the various casinos."

Sylvia's friend in Chicago, Allen Dorfman, was also a key player in the pension fund. Dorfman had become a millionaire in record time after Hoffa had granted him an exclusive on Teamsters insurance plans, for which rank and file members paid three or four times the normal rate of commission. Hoffa and Dorfman had become close in the ensuing years, and they owned several businesses together, including the Jack O'Lantern Lodge in Wisconsin and an oil exploration company in North Dakota, both financed in part from loans from the Fund.

Dorfman wasn't yet privy to the kickbacks Hoffa received, but he made good money from the fund anyway. "It was an unwritten rule," said one investigator. "When you got a loan from the fund, you bought your insurance from Allen Dorfman."

As the fund grew into a billion-dollar behemoth, the American Mafia had what reporter Steven Brill described as, "control of one of the nation's major financial institutions and one of the very largest private sources of real estate investment capital in the world."

And Sylvia was at the center of it. Secret FBI recordings from the early 1960's make it clear that Sylvia was brokering loans on behalf of mafiosi in Detroit, Kansas City, Chicago, and New York. The recordings also make it clear that Sylvia was more than a connection; she was also a counsler and a convincer. Accomodating as he was, Hoffa was far from a rubber stamp; he made loans on his terms and to his advantage. "Jimmy Hoffa is the type of guy you can't bulldog," said Tony Jack's brother, Vito "Billy Jack" Giacalone. "There ain't nobody sharp enough for Jimmy Hoffa, answered Tony Jack. "In this town or any other town. He's going to use everybody. Every SOB in the world."

Sylvia's soft touch, on the other hand, usually got results. "My mother had a way of saying 'Jimmy' that he'd melt," said Chuckie. "And then she would talk to him and he would listen…when Uncle Tony and them couldn't [obtain a loan], they'd come to her and she'd do it. My mother could get Hoffa to do anything the Outfit wanted."

FBI recordings from the Giacalones office at the Home Juice Company—a business they grew with the help of a $500,000 pension fund loan—illustrate how involved and productive Sylvia was with the Mafia's bank:

> Vito Giaclaone: "Mike Polizzi[13] said that he would have never gotten his loan of $630,000 without Jimmy. Mike said, 'Tony got this for me through Sylvia.' Mike said he could have never gotten this loan from nobody, and he wanted to pay ten percent."

> Anthony Giacalone: "Sylvia is the only person in this country that can handle Jimmy Hoffa."

The $630,000 loan Sylvia brokered for Mike Polizzi eventually grew to $1.2 million (about $10.3 million in 2026 dollars) and helped finance the Detroit family's push into the Frontier and Alladin casinos in Las Vegas.

Facilitating Hoffa's relationship with LCN and taking care of his family were not the only duites Sylvia performed for the Teamsters boss. Her days as a front-line salter and organizer were behind her, but she continued to carry out communications and execute administrative tasks on behalf of Local 299, where Sylvia's status as Hoffa's trusted emissary was well understood by the staff. Recordings reveal that Hoffa even had Sylvia sign his name on documents with her initials next to his signature. But Sylvia's union activites went beyond Detroit. "Jimmy gave me the title National Coordinator," said Sylvia in

---

[13] Michael "Big Mike" Polizzi typified Detroit's second generation mafiosi whose fathers sent them to college. Polizzi earned an accounting degree from Syracuse University but remained involved in armed robbery and other rackets.

advance of a Teamsters convention in 1963. Sylvia also spoke regularly with some of Hoffa's many lawyers, including superstar defense attorney Edward Bennet Williams, whose client list included Frank Costello, Frank Sinatra, Joe McCarthy, and Jack Ruby.

If Moe Dalitz was the Godfather of Las Vegas, Jimmy Hoffa was Ceasar himself, or at least that's how he was described by reporters who covered his guest-of-honor appearance at the star-studded grand opening of Caesars Palace in August 1966. By then, Hoffa was preparing to go to prison, but he received a hero's welcome in the city he had helped build. The Desert Inn, Dunes, Stardust, Sahara, Circus Circus, Aladdin, Frontier, Freemont, Four Queens, Hacienda, and Tropicana casinos; the Las Vegas County Club; Sunrise Hospital; the Las Vegas Convention Center, and other real estate developments were all built, bought, or upgraded with money from the Central States Pension Fund. Hoffa used the celebratory occasion to announce that the next multi-million dollar Las Vegas loan would go to the Landmark Tower, the city's first high-rise that featured a revolving casino and restaurant at the top. Sitting next to Hoffa when he made the announcment was Roy Williams, whose tuxedoed attire and jolly expression masked the sheer terror he had experienced in the lead-up to the Landmark loan in Kansas City.

CHAPTER ELEVEN

NICK CIVELLA GETS HIS WAY

"With its billions from the Central States Pension Fund, its tremendous economic leverage, and its immense patronage, the Teamsters union was the pearl of the Mob's oyster. The union was worth spilling blood over."

Investigative journalist James Neff, 1989.

Jimmy Hoffa came back to Kansas City in May 1957 and sat at the head of the table when Roy Williams was honored by the Italian-American service organization UNICO National as man of the year. Dr. James DiRenna was the Kansas City UNICO President at the same time that he held contracts with Locals 41 and 541 for medical treatment of thier members. Roy Williams would later testify how Nick Civella came to receive kickbacks on the arrangement. According to Williams, he had rebuffed Civella's overtures until he was accosted in downtown Kansas City by Thomas "Hiway" Simone and another man, who told him that he would be taken care of if he went along with the plan. But if he didn't, his wife, his two children, and Williams himself would be all be killed.

Williams flew to Detroit and conferred with Jimmy Hoffa, who advised Williams to "do what Nick wants," and raise membership dues to cover the cost. Williams complied.

L to R: Dr. James DiRenna, Roy Williams, and Jimmy Hoffa in Kansas City in 1957.

When Hoffa appointed Roy Williams as a trustee for the Fund, Nick Civella thought he had the inside track to the loan racket. But Williams again hesitated when Civella came calling for loans. Williams then got a crash course in gangster tactics, and one that illustrated the high stakes involved with the Mafia's bank.

After a meeting at Teamsters headquarters on Linwood Boulevard, Roy Williams walked to his car and found two tough-looking men waiting for him. They shoved Williams into the backseat of another car, where two more thugs blindfolded him. After a disorienting 20-minute drive, Williams was marched into an empty warehouse, footsteps echoing ominously. The kidnappers parked Williams on a stool, and when his blindfold was removed, he found himself in a darkened room staring into a white-hot spotlight. "You're going to have to cooperate better with Mr. Civella," came a voice out of the darkness. "If you don't cooperate, were going to kill your children, and your wife. You'll be the last to go."

Williams again sought the counsel of Jimmy Hoffa, and Hoffa again advised Williams to appease Civella. Williams acquiesced, and Nick Civella became a major powerbroker in the Fund. From that point on, Nick would get his loans, including $5 million[14] for Civella's piece of the Landmark Tower in Las Vegas. And when supplicants from around the country came to Roy Williams for a loan, he told them to "go see my friend in Kansas City."

Sylvia's old friend, Nick Civella, in his later years.

---

[14] Approximately $42 million in 2026 dollars

Civella made sure that Williams got a share of the spoils, and more than once took extreme measures to make sure Williams stayed in power. As the 1960 Local 41 elections approached, a KC union dissident named Jake Henderson was busy speaking out against Williams and Hoffa. On the night of April 13, 1959, Henderson was inside his home at 415 Paseo writing the latest in series of letters condemning Hoffa and Williams. Outside, an assaliant embodying the ghost of Pellegrino Scaglia snuck up to an open window with a shotgun and blasted away at Mr. Henderson. Henderson survived the shooting with 65 pellets in both legs.

Hoffa returned to Kansas City in November, 1960 to support Roy Williams in his bid for reelection to the presidency of Local 41. Hoffa assured Williams's victory by disqualifying the only man to file against Williams. While the election was under way, the Linwood Boulevard parking lot of IBT headquarters again became the scene of mayhem when O.B. Eloe, president of Local 552 and a potential rival to the Williams ticket, was attacked in a savage beating that tore his left ear from his head. Thomas Hutson, another dissident who was close to shotgun victim Jake Henderson, was also beaten by unknown assailiants. The fates of these men were typical of those of many other brave union rebels who were assaulted or killed for standing up to coruption, challenging the establishment, or refusing to knuckle under.

Another such man was Stanton Gladden, a battalion chief with the Kansas City Fire Department and the president of Local 42 of the International Firefighters Union. In July 1959, Teamsters Local 774 began an organizing drive to bring the Firefighters into the Teamsters. The Mafia-infiltrated Kansas City Council supported the Teamsters in what Gladden labled as an attempt to "politicize the department as a source of patronage."

Jackson County Prosecuter William Collet commented on the machinations that involved the Teamsters, the Mafia, and the Democratic political machine in Kansas City, "There is talk Civella takes instructions from James Hoffa. The Teamsters and the North Side organization work together…There is an alliance in an attempt to organize the Fire Department…there is no question about it."

Battalion Chief Gladden resisted tremendous pressure to join the Teamsters, but he was willing to meet with anyone who might help resolve the conflict. On June 2, 1960, Gladden met with Cork Civella at the Pickwick building at 10th and McGee. Civella told Gladden that he believed he had enough political pull to make Gladden fire chief if he would get behind the Teamsters. Gladden wasn't interested, and told Civella as much.

On February 9, 1961, at 6:15 a.m., Gladden exited his home at 8000 E. 83rd Street and got into his 1958 Plymouth. Gladden's two sons were blown from their beds when when their father turned the ignition and the car exploded. The hood of the car sailed over the house and landed 200 feet away in the backyard. Gladden survived the explosion with a pair of broken ankles, but the case was never solved.

But that wasn't the end of Teamster associated violence in Kansas City. Floyd Hayes was another one of the original peckerwood racketeers who dominated the KC Teamsters before the Outfit's takeover. His criminal record went back to 1917 and included arrests for stolen cars, liquor law violations, and assaults. Like Roy Williams, Hayes was an old friend of Jimmy Hoffa's who had helped Hoffa in the early days of organizing Local 299 in Detroit. In 1959, Hayes went to prison for 18 months for tax evasion, but Roy Williams made sure that Hayes collected his Local 41 salary while he served his time. In 1962, Hayes, Williams and four other Teamsters were charged with conspiracy to steal union funds in a scheme involving kickbacks, bill padding, and payoffs. Williams was found not guity, but Hayes and the others were convicted and Hayes received a four-year sentence.

Roy Williams (L), and Floyd Hayes

Nobody expected the hardened Hayes to cooperate with the FBI, but the old man was eager to stay out of prison, and cooperate he did. Hayes had more than enough information to bury Roy Williams and rob Nick Civella of his most valuable asset.

On June 11, 1964, Floyd Hayes and his wife finished an evening of bowling at King Louie East. In the parking lot, Hayes's wife waited at a safe distance while Hayes went to activate the remote-controlled starter he had cautiously installed in his car. But Hayes had misjudged the method the mobsters would use to get rid of him. A car sped into the lot and a shotgun emerged from the passenger window. The gunman felled Hayes with one blast, exited the car and delivered another point-blank shot. The driver then aimed at Hayes's wife and shot her in the torso. She survived with only a superficial wound, but her husband was dead and Roy Williams would continue his rise in the IBT, taking Nick Civella with him every step of the way.

CHAPTER TWELVE

ARSON AND SURVEILLANCE

"We put microphones into the headquarters of the mob across the country. We had scores of them. We knew what the mob was doing on a daily basis."

FBI agent William Roemer

On the evening of July 16, 1959, while Chuckie was at a friend's ranch in Jackson Hole, Wyoming and Marie and the kids were visiting family in Kansas City, Sylvia left the Bloomfield Township residence she had shared with John Paris and now shared with Chuckie's family. She drove a short distance and joined other neighbors at a town meeting. Less than one hour later the interior of Sylvia's home was engulfed in flames. After they extinguished the blaze, firefighters found four empty five-gallon fuel oil cans in the living room and upstairs bedrooms. Investigators determined that the floors of the rooms had been drenched with oil and they quickly ruled the fire as arson. "We don't know why the fire was set," said arson investigator Oramel O'Farrell. "But we know it was no accident."

Sylvia told reporters that recent attempts by her son to organize city employees in suburban Dearborn might have been the motive for the blaze. "He got many threats," said Sylvia. "People who said they were from Dearborn called and said they would beat him up or kill him if he didn't lay off. He called them cranks and laughed at the calls, but they worried me and his wife."

When Chuckie returned to the house he was accompanied by hockey legend Gordie Howe, a family friend who lived in the neighborhood and was an idol to Chuckie's young son, who would grow up to work for the National Hockey League in Kansas City. Howe told reporters he was shocked at the crime: "Those guys really play rough. I thought hockey was rough but we're a bunch of patsies compared to something like this."

Sylvia's connections to both the Teamsters and the Laundry Workers caused arson investigator O'Farrell to comment, "The way it stands now, it is a hot potato. Whether it dovetails into the Kierdorf case is a question." O'Farrell was refering to the firebombing of a laundry plant that had taken place less than a year earlier. In that incident, one of the suspects, a Teamster named Frank Kierdorf, caught fire and burned to death.

A typical Hoffa foot soldier, Kierdorf serves as an example of how Hoffa assembled his army of business agents, who were to the Teamsters what street soldiers were to the Mafia. Kierdorf and his uncle, Herman Kierdorf, had been armed robbery professionals until they both landed in prison on seperate cases. Hoffa assisted with their paroles and gave both the Kierdorfs jobs with the Teamsters when they were released, gaining himself two loyal lieutenants who would organize workers, burn businesses, or bust heads at Hoffa's will. Hoffa had such men as far away as Puerto Rico, and any mobster who might have been tempted to muscle him had Hoffa's large crew of loyalists to consider. It was an extra layer of protection that helped neutralize the type of intimidation tactics the Civella Family used on Roy Williams in Kansas City.

On August 4, 1958, the Keirdorfs and one other man firebombed the Latreille Cleaning Company in Flint, Michigan, where Frank Keirdorf acted as a buisness agent for Teamsters Local 332. Unfortunatley for Frank, he dropped his flashlight and his exit was delayed while he tried to recover it. The device ignited and Frank caught fire. Hours later, he was dead.

Frank Kierdorf

The Kierdorfs had both been called before the McClellen Committee, where they answered every one of Robert Kennedy's questions with an invocation of their Fifth Ammendment rights. Hoffa was scheduled testify the day after Frank Kierdorf burned to death. Kennedy peppered Hoffa with questions about the Keirdorfs, Hoffa's hiring of them, and whether or not Hoffa had ordered them to torch the Latreille laundry.

According to Joe Franco, who introduced Sylvia to John Paris, Hoffa did in fact order the arson. Franco concluded that Hoffa had arranged it as a favor to Sylvia's admirer Moe Dalitz. According to Franco, the laundry tycoon wanted to "send a message to the guys that owned the plants and the whole industry that they were being organized and they'd better not make any trouble."

The Teamsters/Laundry Workers nexus between the Kierdorf case and Sylvia's fire was intriguing to investigators, but no evidence of a conspiracy surfaced. The fire at Sylvia's house caused an estimated $35,000 in damages plus the loss of cash and jewelry that Sylvia had reported stolen. Two insurance companies witheld Sylvia's claims as they conducted their own investigations. The FBI suspected that Tony Giacalone was involved in the crime. They interviewed Oramel O'Farrell, who told agents that the residence was completely locked when firefighters arrived. Sylvia eventually filed suit against both insurance companies as they witheld payment into the following year. No fingerprints were found on the oil cans, and the crime was never solved.

***

Far from Detroit, events unfolding in Cuba were impacting the fortunes of the American Mafia, including some close associates of Jimmy Hoffa who had been either expelled from the island or imprisoned by the new Castro regime. The gambling and vice paradise the mobsters had built in alliance with the previous government led by Fulgencio Batista was in shambles, and the the mob was incensed at what they perceived as a double-cross by Fidel Castro. In the months leading up to Castro's overthrow of Batista, the Mafia had hedged their bets in Cuba by working with the CIA to send clandestine shipments of weapons to both sides in the conflict. Multiple sources including Dan Moldea have implicated Hoffa in the plots: "Strong evidence points to the fact that the original middleman between the CIA and the American underworld was Jimmy Hoffa, who used the union's financial machinery for arms sales to both sides in the Cuban Revolution," wrote Moldea. The relationship led to the CIA/Mafia conspiracies to assasinate Fidel Castro. Those plans failed, but the stage was set for the unholy alliance to morph into the origins of what some investigators believe to be the conspiracy that murdered President John F. Kennedy.

Sylvia was certainly never implicated in the Kennedy assasination, but her proximity to Hoffa and the Mafia did place her in the files of the House Select Committee on Assassinations, also known as the Church Committee. Among the myriad documents preserved in the in the committee's record are FBI transcripts of secret recordings made while Robert Kennedy was Attorney General. Without warrants and in contempt of the Constitution, the FBI had broken into the homes and businesses of hundreds of people suspected of organized crime activities and installed hidden microphones.

In Detroit, the FBI bugged the Giaclaone brothers office at the Home Juice Company, a beverege distribution firm that Tony Jack won in a dice game and grew with the help of a half-million dollar Teamsters loan. The business had about 150 cars and trucks and provided Tony Jack with a $45,000 yearly salary. Giaclone also had an interest in the Macomb Manufacturing Company, which had a lucrative contract with the Ford Motor Company.

But the real money came from the rackets Giacalone was supervising. After Detroit boss Joe Zerilli was promoted to replace New York's Joe Profaci[15] on the national ruling Mafia commission, Zerrilli appointed Tony Jack as his street boss and mouthpiece. It made Giacalone the busiest, most-feared mobster in the city. It also made him the primary target of the Detroit FBI, who noticed that Tony Jack was spending more time with Sylvia. On June 16, 1960, an agent with the FBI attempted to interview Sylvia about Tony Jack, but the *Omerta*-bound Sylvia, "would not admit knowing Anthony Giaclaone and had nothing to say concerning him."

Tony Jack seemed to have been carrying a torch for Sylvia since the days when her relationship with Frank Coppola made her off-limits to a youngster like himself. After John Paris died, Sylvia and Tony finally consummated what had probably been percolating since the days when she brokered Giacalone's alliance with Jimmy Hoffa. If it was out of character for a mobster to take an older mistress—Sylvia was four years his senior—Tony Jack didn't seem to mind. Recordings illustrated the sincere emotions Tony Jack felt for Sylvia, but there were also tactical advantages to the affair;

---

[15] Profaci's two daughters were married to the sons of Black Bill Tocco and Joseph Zerilli in Detroit.

Sylvia was still acting as the go-between for Giaclaone and Hoffa, and Sylvia was still, in Tony Jack's words, "the only person who can handle Jimmy Hoffa."

Sylvia's beau, Anthony "Tony Jack" Giacalone, in the 1960's

As a potential key to both the street boss of Detroit and the Attorney General's archenemy Jimmy Hoffa, Sylvia was one of the most tantalizing targets in the nation for FBI agents. In January 1961, agents broke into in her new residence on the 6th floor of the Alden Park Manor apartments at 1550 East Jefferson Avenue on Detroit's Gold Coast and installed a bug in her living room.

Sylvia's grandson remembered her waterfront apartment as the place where he always got bacon for breakfast. "Nonna Sylvia was a great cook," said Chuckie's namesake. "The best breaded veal ever. Sauce, pasta…everything she made was good."

Tony Giaclone would have agreed. Sylvia is on tape making her lover meals of steak, lamb chops, crab salad, cheese souffles, and fried chicken. Her attention to cuisine was matched by a fastidious devotion to cleanliness, as evidenced by daily vacuuming and instructions to workers hired to wash her walls and clean her drapes and furniture.

"Her apartment was nice," remembered her grandson. "There was marble in the lobby. You could see the Detroit River through her windows, and we used to watch the boat races from there. I didn't know the feds were listening to us in her apartment. I didn't know nothin' from nothin.' To me, she was just Nonna Sylvia. She was a very classy dresser, and I always thought she was very beautiful. She always took me and my sister shopping for school clothes. She was there for Christmas and on birthdays, she was at my first communion, my graduations…My dad didn't make it to some of these things because he was always away travelling with Hoffa, but Nonna Sylvia would come with my mom. She was just a very classy woman. I went to Miami with her for a week when I was about 11-years-old. She made me feel like I was older. Things like trusting me to go to the pool by myself. She made me feel older and important."

L to R: Maryann O'Brien, her son, Chuck O'Brien, and Chuck's grandmother, Sylvia, at Chuck's 8th grade graduation in 1967.

The FBI's survellience of Sylvia included interviews with her neighbors, one of whom said that Sylvia, who was 5'2," and 124-pounds in 1963, "looked like gypsy and always wore tight torcador pants." Another neighbor told the FBI how Jimmy Hoffa and Anthony Giacalone would both use the service elevator when they visited Sylvia's apartment. A tenant on the eigth floor told of an apartment rented by "a very well dressed man" who used the apartment only occasionaly, did not stay overnight, and, "always tried to sneak in and out without any of the neighbors seeing him." According to this tenant, Sylvia often went into this apartment and had conversations with one or two other men, "in a foreign language, probably Italian."

"Nonna Sylvia did speak some Italian," said her grandson. "She wanted me to speak Italian, so she hired a guy from Berlitz to come to the house and tutor me three days a week. She made us sit for a professional painter and do portraits…typical grandmother stuff. She didn't drink or smoke or gamble, and neither did my father. She was a very strong woman. When Nonna Sylvia was mad at my dad, she called him 'Charles.' I think my dad was more scared of her than he was of Jimmy Hoffa or Tony Giaclaone."

After John Paris died in 1957, Hoffa insisted that Local 129 of the Laundry Workers Union keep Sylvia on the payroll for two years. With that time now expired, Tony Jack stepped up his own financial support. In 1963 he bought two brand new Pontiac Grand Prix's, a gold one for himself and a gray one for Sylvia. Giaclaone would later have the roofs of both cars converted to leather. But the vehicle registration on Sylvia's Grand Prix showed that she wasn't wholly dependant on Tony Jack. Sylvia's Pontiac was registered to "S. Paris Productions, 560 Book Building. FBI documents described the business as a talent agency "supplying specialty acts for conventions." Sylvia was also reported as the owner of the Wayne Window Cleaning Company at 151 West Jefferson Street, a business she had inherited from her late husband. Sylvia also drew a salary from one of Allen Dorfman's insurance companies. "She's one of their representatives," said Giacalone. "She's on their steady payroll there in Chicago."

Between her own income and the support of Tony Jack, Sylvia lived the type of comfortable life befitting a Mafia mistress. Giacalone is on record paying Sylvia's rent, and shipments of French perfume to Sylvia's address were probably gifts from her lover. But whatever Tony Jack did for Sylvia, it was well worth the cost: "Sylvia is your key to Jimmy Hoffa," said Giacalone in a recorded conversation. "What she has done for us and vice versa in business—there is no money that could pay for it."

CHAPTER THIRTEEN

SYLVIA'S SLUGGER SON

"I had been struggling with something in me that told me I had to kill someone for over a year, but I didn't know who. Then a voice told me, 'You have to kill Jimmy Hoffa.'"

Warren Swanson, 1962

While the FBI spied on Sylvia and the Giacalones, a Detroit Teamsters rebel named Melvin Angel did the unthinkable and worked openly against Jimmy Hoffa's reelection to the presidency of Detroit's Local 299, an office Hoffa maintined along with his postion as Internationl IBT President. The fued came to a head in Hoffa's Detroit office when Angel confronted Hoffa over a car hauler's contract. According to Angel, Hoffa charged across the room, grabbed him by the throat, and began strangling him. The commotion caught the attention of Rolland McMaster, a 6' 5" gorilla of a Teamster whom Robert Kennedy accuratley labeld as one of Hoffa's "roving emmissaries of voilence." McMaster was known for starting fights and winning them, but in this case he broke up the assault and escorted Angel to the parking lot. Angel immediately reported the incident to police and passed a lie detector test. Two days later, he returned to the union hall with two detectives to get a witness statement from McMaster.

A crowd gathered in the halls as McMaster denied witnessing the fight. Chuckie O'Brien sprang out of the crowd and attacked Melvin Angel. The detectives tried to intervene, but McMaster threw both of them against a wall and kept them at bay while the crowd clasped hands and formed a protective circle around the ground fight raging between Angel and O'Brien. McMaster decided it was enough and broke up the fight. Angel and the detectives couldn't run away fast enough. McMaster and O'Brien were eventually indicted for obstruction of justice and assault and battery, but with William Bufalino representing them, the charges were dismissed because the police had entered the union hall without a search warrant.

It wouldn't be long before Sylvia's son attacked another man on behalf of his boss. The incident took place on December 5, 1962, in Nashville, Tennessee while Hoffa was on trial for extorting money from a trucking company. It was Robert Kennedy's latest attempt to finally convict his sworn enemy, and Hoffa was throwing every resource the union could muster at winning an aquittal. The trial lasted forty-two days, and top Teamsters officials flocked to Nashville to rally around their leader and assist with his defense. Hoffa's legal team included Detroit jukebox local president Bill Bufalino; Frank Ragano, a Tampa attorney who also represented Hoffa's close underworld ally Santo Trafficante; and Morris Shenker from St. Louis, who also represented Nick Civella and would borrow more than $100 million from the Fund for various projects including the Dunes Hotel and Casino in Las Vegas.

On December 5, 1962, a man wearing a full-length raincoat walked into the courtroom, made straight for Jimmy Hoffa and began firing a pellet gun at point blank range. Hoffa was hit in neck, forearms and shoulders, but the pellets didn't stop Hoffa from lunging at his assailant and punching him to the ground. Alarmed and enraged, Chuckie O'Brien pounced on the man and delieverd a beating so savage that a U.S. Marshal had to strike Chuckie to get him to stop. "A deputy ran over," said Hoffa, "and, instead of grabbing the guy who tried to kill me, the dumb bastard started banging O'Brien over the head with his gun butt to get him off the guy."

Hoffa continued, "It turned out that the guy's name was Warren Swanson, a drifter who had worked on and off as a dishwasher. He was nuttty as a fruitcake, saying he had a 'message from a higher power' to kill Jimmy Hoffa."

Warren Swanson after Chuckie O'Brien beat him up

Chuckie explained his violent reaction to the shooting, "I wanted to kill him because I thought he killed the Old Man." It was a demonstration of loyalty that had Hoffa beaming, "My man O'Brien held that fellow down," said Hoffa, brimming with pride. "I raised that kid."

Phone records obtained by the FBI show Sylvia's number blowing up with calls to and from Nashville on the day of the incident. Everything about Sylvia's values suggest that she shared Hoffa's pride in her son, and of course Uncle Tony would aslo have been delighted. For a while at least, Chuckie was a hero.

On December 23, 1962, the jury announced that it was unable to reach a unanimous verdict. It was Robert Kennedy's fifth defeat from Hoffa since 1957. But Kennedy had an ace in the hole. It turned out that one member of Hoffa's Nashville entourage, a Louisiana IBT official named Edward Grady Partin, was a snitch. Partin began working with the Justice Department in advance of the trial and had been feeding information to the government about attempts to bribe jurors.

But that wasn't all.

In September, 1962, fourteen months before President Kennedy was assasinated, Partin told two Louisiana law enforcement officials that one month earlier, Hoffa had told him of a plan to kill Robert Kennedy by using a single gunman who would shoot Kennedy from a distance with a high powered rifle while Kennedy rode in his convertible somewhere in the Southern United States. "Somebody needs to bump that son of a bitch off," Partin accused Hoffa of saying. "Bobby Kennedy has got to go."

CHAPTER FOURTEEN

"I'LL TAKE CARE OF EVERYTHING."

"My mother was a saint."

Chuckie O'Brien

Chuckie's bravery in Nashville earned him a greater role as a conduit between Hoffa and the mob. Each of the men Chuckie sat down with was a point of pride for Sylvia's son: Accardo, Giancana, Ricca, Glimco, and Rosanova in Chicago; Tony "Ducks" Corallo in New York; Meyer Lansky in Florida; the Civella brothers and Willie Cammisano in Kansas City; Russell Bufalino in Pennsylvania; Carlos Marcello in New Orleans; Tony Pro in New Jersey, and practically every made man in Detroit. The list represented the upper echelon of what Sylvia's son called "The Company," and it was a source of prestige for a kid from the North End of Kansas City. Not even Nick Civella had as many meetings with high level LCN contacts as the half-Irish son of Charlie Binaggio's wheelman.

Sylvia was buoyed by her son's progress, but in the early 1960's, the men in her life required what must have been exhausting amounts of emotional energy from Sylvia. In June, 1961, her father, Joseph Pagano, died of a heart attack at age 78. After his retirement as a track inspector, Joe and Maggie had moved from Independence Avenue to 609 Forest. The native Sicilian had lived 70 of his 78 years in Kansas City and stayed out of trouble the whole time.

Not so for the other men that Sylvia loved. In addition to his indictment for the assault on Melvin Angel, Chuckie was also charged with receiving stolen property salvaged from a freighter that had sunk in the Detroit River. Along with Detroit mobster and boxing racketeer Sam Finazzo, Chuckie stood accused of taking seven tons of marble and other items from the Detroit Customs Terminal. Chuckie was later found guilty and sentenced to one year and one day in prison.[16] Chuckie was also charged with throwing rocks at the moving car of an owner of an air freight business that Local 299 was trying to organize.

Detroit boxing boss Sam Finazzo was Chuckie O'Brien's partner in the freighter cargo escapade and brother-in-law to Joe Zerilli.

---

[16] Chuckie appealed his conviction in the theft from the Detroit Customs Terminal to the Supreme Court, where it was vacated due to the illegality of the microphone at the Home Juice Company. "I didn't steal nothing and that wasn't a bonded warehouse," Chuckie told his stepson. "They said they were going to throw that shit away and I bought it."

Jimmy Hoffa was at war with the government and would soon face two trials: one for jury tampering in the Nashville case and another for receiving kickbacks on $20 million in pension fund loans.

Tony Giacalone was deeply immersed in a tumultous underworld that kept him on a tightrope spanning violent death and prison. He would soon be indicted for income tax evasion and he was preparing to go to war with Sylvia's old associate, Santo Perrone.

Cockeyed Sam was now part of a faction of old-timers in the Detroit Family who were hostile to Tony Jack. When Joe Zerilli had appointed Giacalone as street boss, he bestowed him with broad authority that extended to older men. Santo Perrone and others didn't like taking orders from a man young enough to be their son.

After avoiding prosecution in the shootings of UAW leaders Walter and Victor Ruether, Perrone continued wreaking violence on the streets of Detroit. Investigators believed that Perrone was responsible for a series of five bombings in 1960-61. Explosives were uncharacteristic of the Detroit Outfit, whose leaders usually ordered more discreet methods, but the vicious old strikebreaker was known for being uncontrollable, and he had little use for subtlety.

Santo Perrone got a taste of his own medicine after Joe Zerilli and his *consiglieri*, Papa John Priziola, granted Giaclaone's request to kill the 69-year-old man. On January 19, 1963, Perrone left the car wash he owned and walked two doors down to the Aladdin Cleaners & Dyers Company, where his car was parked. A pair of policemen happened to be driving by when Perrone turned his ignition and triggered a deafening explosion that hurled pieces of the car onto the roofs of neighboring buildings. The policemen spun into the parking lot just as Perrone fell out of his car. Thanks to his habit of leaving the car door open when he started it—a discipline he practiced for just such an occasion—the bomb did not kill Cockeyed Sam, but it blew his right leg off and mangled his left leg below the knee.

The Giaclaone crew later caught a Perrone soldier attempting to plant a bomb under Tony Jack's car. That man was later killed, and Perrone met the same fate as Sylvia's uncle, Mariano Scaglia, when he was stripped of his membership in the secret society.

In the trunk of Perrone's car, police found a .22 rifle with a telescopic sight, a 20-gauge double-barreled shotgun, ammunition, and four bottles of whiskey.

The activites of the men in her life made her own safety and freedom uncertain, but Sylvia seems to have accepted the risks without much complaint. Assiting such men was the life she had chosen. But even if she coped well with the drama and the danger, the sheer workload associated with her son, her boss, and her lover would've tested the patience of a saint. Even so, Sylvia's biggest source of stress was another woman: Josephine Hoffa.

Jospehine's alcoholism was now severe, and Sylvia was charged with managing it. Josephine was a bona-fide lush, prone to embarrassing displays of inebriation and a constant source of exasperation for Sylvia, who couldn't even leave Josephine alone in her apartment with her maid: "JOSEPHINE apparently drunk and giving drinks to [Sylvia's] cleaning woman," reported the FBI.

But even when Josephine was sober, she lacked the grit and productivity Sylvia was known for. Afflicted with undulant fever, Josephine's fragile health and acute alcoholism rendered her incapable of managing her own affairs. Sylvia's caretaker role included errands, medical appointments, paperwork, scheduling, public relations, and event planning. At the 1961 IBT convention, Jospehine hosted 2,000 Teamster wives at a luncheon that Sylvia planned. Sylvia also travelled extensively with Josephine, visiting 29 different states in 1962 alone.

Sylvia's role as the glue that kept the Hoffa family together was apparent at Barbara Hoffa's wedding in 1961. The event featured 300 guests and all the earmarks of a traditional mob wedding, including an eight-foot-tall, eighteen-layer wedding cake, flowers galore, and a king-for-the-night father of the bride. Sylvia made all the arrangements, and her daughter-in-law was matron of honor while her grandchildren acted as ring-bearer and flower girl.

Sylvia's grandchildren with "Uncle Jimmy" at Barbara Hoffa's wedding

When Hoffa finally decided to commit Josephine to a sanitorium after she suffered a nervous breakdown, it fell to Sylvia to not only facilitate the stay, but to host Josephine's mother at her apartment and wait on the elderly woman's many needs. "You're lucky you have Josephine and Jimmy," Sylvia told Josephine's mother. "God gave them to you. Just think if you didn't have nobody. You got us."

There were also periods of time when Sylvia looked after Jimmy Hoffa's mother. When his mother was sick while Hoffa was on trial in 1964, Sylvia called Hoffa, and, according to Tony Giacalone, "told him his mother was aching for him. Says, 'Your poor mother would like to hear your voice.' He says, 'I don't want to hear about my mother. I'm on trial and I don't want to hear about nobody.' He says, 'You know how to handle it, you do the best you can.'"

The Giacalones typically spoke highly of Hoffa, even when they thought no one was listening, but snubbing his mother was a bridge too far for the Sicilian brothers: "What kind of a motherfucker is this, he don't want his mother?" asked an incredulous Vito Giacalone.

"This motherfucker is an atheist…this bastard," answered Tony Jack.

Sylvia was an attentive, unselfish caretaker, and her ability to remain patient while multi-tasking comes across as admirable and endearing. Transcripts from the secret microphone in her apartment revealed that "I'll take care of everything," was a phrase Sylvia used often—even habitually--with family, friends, and business associates. But the strain of being a rock to so many needy people was catching up to her. During her whirlwind summer of 1963, Sylvia called her doctor to report that she "went to lie down and the bed started spinning around at 100 miles per hour and I couldn't lift my head up."

Despite the demands Josephine Hoffa placed on her, Sylvia's affection for Josphine was sincere. A recorded conversation concerning Josephine's sanitorium stay reveal Sylvia's genuine concern for her friend: "I mean, is it a nice place?" Sylvia demanded to know. "What do they have there? Does she have her own room and bath? Does she have a TV room? What about the food, what do they do? And do they have outside grounds where she can walk? I want them to check her from her head to her toes."

Recordings also captured heartwarming phone calls between Sylvia and Josephine after Josephine checked into the facility: "I love you, Josephine, I don't want anything to happen to you…That's why Chuck is there and I'm not there yet. And I got robes and I got nightgowns and everything that you need, so don't worry about that. I love you and take it easy and I'll take care of everything. I don't want you to cry. You hear honey? Are you listening to me? And I love you. Alright, bye."

"A lot of people would shit on Ma Jo behind her back," said Chuckie. "Once my mother went over and told one of them, "If you don't stop that shit, I'll knock your fucking head across the street."

Sylvia and Josephine Hoffa

Prior to her nervous breakdown, Josephine had often been a third wheel with Sylvia and Tony Jack on dates at the Living Room Lounge, a Detroit supper club at 58 Lothrop Street that Giaclaone had an interest in. Sylvia's beau was thoughtful and generous with Sylvia's best friend. He sent steak and lobster dinners to Josephine while she was hospitalized, and once admonished Sylvia for not arranging for a car to pick up Josephine at the airport. But Giaclaone's idea of helping Josephine took a scandalous and self-serving turn after Sylvia had reached her wits end with her charge. "I could have beat the shit out of her today," said Sylvia to Tony Jack. "I've had it, Tony. I must have nerves made of steel. I have to do fucking everything…If she is going to take all them tranquilizers and then she is going to drink with them, what can I do for her?"

"You can't watch her all the time," said Tony Jack. "Because this woman is going to put you out of your mind."

So Tony added a fourth wheel. Anthony Cimini was a Giaclaone pal who ended up in a torrid, 18-month affair with Jimmy Hoffa's wife. And when that affair ended, Gaiclaone facilitated another affair for Jospehine with his brother, Vito "Billy Jack" Giaclaone. It was brazen, but hardly less so than his own affair with Sylvia, whose whole family was close to the Giaclones. Sylvia even shared a dental appointment with Tony Jack's wife, Zina, at the height of her affair with Zina's husband.

Facilitating and documenting affairs was a power play frequently used by mobsters to gain leverage over useful people. Blackmail was but one of many advantages gained through illicit sex. Giacalone would have time to ponder the myriad ways he might exploit Jospehine's affairs, but he was at least somewhat concerned about potential fallout. An FBI summary referencing Josephine's affair with Anthony Cimini documented a conversation at Home Juice: "GIACALONE stated that he had all kinds of respect for JIMMY HOFFA and this might just be some type of thing to cause dissension between JIMMY and TONY."

Jimmy and Josephine Hoffa

Giacalone needen't have worried. His relationship with Hoffa remained intact even after Hoffa found out about Jo's affair with Anthony Cimini and alledgedly talked to Joe Zerilli about whacking Cimini. Hoffa and Tony Jack remained friends, Tony Jack continued to help Sylvia with Jospehine, and Sylvia continued to facilitate the many favors that Hoffa and Giacalone did for each other. Giacalone gave Hoffa gifts of custom-made clothing that the dapper mobster hoped would improve Hoffa's proletarian appearance, which included off-the-rack suits worn with white socks because Hoffa's feet were allergic to dyes. Tony Jack had his tailor make socks for Hoffa that were white at the feet but dyed at the ankles. After Tony Jack was arrested in June 1963 for bribing a cop, Hoffa paid a $15,000 bribe to the judge for an eventual dismissal. And when Hoffa needed a solution for promoting a favored Teamster official over another one whom he couldn't afford to offend, Tony Jack provided him with a double-sided coin that Hoffa flipped while the two hopefuls witnessed the "fair" contest.

But even though his relationship with Hoffa survived, the affair between Josephine Hoffa and Anthony Cimini backfired on Giacalone in more ways than one. Detroit Family elder Pete Licavoli and Licavoli's right-hand man, Mike Rubino, found out about the affair and confronted Tony Jack. Anthony Cimini worked for their crew, and Rubino and Licavoli were both affronted with the implications of the affair. Giacalone held his ground and demanded to know the source of their information, which they refused. "I says, 'Mike, let's be man enough huh?,'" Tony Jack told his brother. "I says, 'when did you ever keep anything away from me or me keep anything from you? You're looking at me like I'm an outsider. If somebody asks me a question, this is the way I was taught, I says, by Pete Corrado when he made me. Never lie to a friend of ours.'"

When Tony Zerilli stepped in to mediate the dispute and make a judgement, the FBI got a crash course in the inner workings and ways of the Detroit Family as Zerilli spoke freely and philosophically over the hidden microphone at Home Juice.

But that wasn't the only paydirt the FBI got from the affair. Zerilli ruled in Tony Jack's favor and Licavoli and Rubino gave up their source, which turned out to be the FBI's own surveillence report that described Cimini and Josephine entering a motel room together. Thanks to the mobsters own discussions on the hidden microphone, the FBI had discovered a leak in the legal division of their Detroit office.

In another ironic twist to the story, agents listening in on an illegal microphone authorized by Robert Kennedy heard the mobsters tell how the corrupted FBI legal division employee told their go-between that the FBI, "have orders from Bobby Kennedy that the Italian Syndicate individuals are to be arrested even if they had to be framed."

In yet another twist, President Kennedy was himself involved in a mobbed-up affair with alarming implications. Even while Tony Jack was making a cuckhold out Hoffa, Chicago boss Sam Giancana was knowingly and enthusiastically sharing a mistresses, Judith Campbell, with President Kennedy.[17] Giancana would later become a suspect in President Kennedy's assassination along with Jimmy Hoffa.

***

While Tony Jack was busy bombing Santo Perrone and taking over the numbers racket from Detroit's African American syndicate, his wife's cousin, Tony Provenzano, was

---

[17] Many sources also claim that JFK and Sam Giancana shared another mistress: Marilyn Monroe

busy becoming the highest-paid union official in the world as he drew multiple bloated salaries from various positions he had obtained with Hoffa's help. Tony Pro's rise was also facilitated by violence, including the 1961 killing of Anthony Castellito, a union official who had challenged Provenzano's presidency of New Jersey Local 560. Other challengers and reformers were also killed or hospitalized as Provenzano solidified his power as both a Teamsters boss and *caporegime* in the Genovese crime family.

Tony Pro and Tony Jack would later conspire to kill Jimmy Hoffa, but for now the three men enjoyed a mutually beneficial friendship that Sylvia had nurtured into something familial with her son's foster dad and two "uncles." Her connection to Tony Pro extended her national influence beyond the Midwest and brought her and Chuckie clout on the East Coast. In a manner befitting her status, Sylvia travelled with Tony and Vito Giaclaone to New Jersey in February, 1963, to attend a testimonial dinner and dance honoring Tony Provenzano at the Hotel Essex House in Newark. Like all Teamsters testimonials, it was a high-class affair, and *Facci* was resplendant in her evening gown and towering hairdo. She mixed and mingled with pillar-of-the-community types and leading powerbrokers in labor and organized crime. But the tuxedoes and laudatory speeches masked the dark realities of Provenzano's reign. Only a few months later, while Tony Pro was on trial for receiving labor peace payoffs from a trucking company, a Local 560 dissident named Walter Glockner was shot to death outside his New Jersey home. The night before the murder, Glockner had announced at a shop stewards meeting that he was going to "fight Tony Pro until they put me in a pine box."

Sylvia with her close friend, Anthony "Tony Pro" Provenzano, and Provenzano's wife, Maria, in Miami Beach, 1957.

Just as Tony Pro was Sylvia's best connection in the East, Allen Dorfman was her primary link to Chicago. The man with an exclusive on Teamsters insurance plans was becoming a major player in the Central States Pension Fund, and his power grew in step with the burgioning billions of dollars held in the Fund. Like his fellow Jewish racketeer Moe Dalitz, Dorfman cherished his connection to Sylvia and the power it yielded. He kept her on his payroll, and he used her as a link to both Hoffa and the Detroit LCN: "TONY GIACALONE says that while she was in Chicago, Allen Dorfman asked SYLVIA to check with the boys in Detroit and see if they wanted to buy his [Miami Beach] BLAIR HOUSE."

On September 5, 1963 at 7:55 a.m., Sylvia placed a call to Allen Dorfman in Chicago. The microphone in her apartment captured only her side of the conversation, but Sylvia's statements illustrate her closeness to Dorfman, her devotion to Jimmy Hoffa, and the take-charge attitude she took in her role as Hoffa's representative and liason to some of the most powerful men in his orbit:

> "Hello, honey. How are you?... I just talked to Jimmy. He called me. I told him I'd take care of everything.

> "Don't make me laugh. I don't care. I'd do anything in the world for that man. You know that.

> "Now, this is why I'm calling you: Michael is coming in there. You know Mike. Jimmy was supposed to be there in Lewis's office. He wanted to go Wednesday but he called and said he had to go to court, so would you check on it? He left there at 7:15 and he doesn't know that Jimmy's not going to be there. And that jerk better take care of it, 'cause that's orders from headquarters.

> "All right, honey."

Sylvia's close friend and business associate, Allen Dorfman, in 1981

Sylvia's assertivness when conducting business became downright ornery during the Summer of 1963 when caregiver duties to both Josephine and her visiting mother were added to Sylvia's head-spinning schedule. The wits-end frustration she had expressed to Tony Jack boiled over in a phone conversation that captured Sylvia going full gangster on a secretary at Local 299 who Sylvia believed was holding back a check that she was due. "Tell her I'll break her fucking neck! Watch her, she'll get excited when I say that. I'm in a fighting mood. That redhead; I'm going to break her fucking neck. Wait till you see her. I'm going to throw her out of the door. If she's got what I want, she's through. I'm going to come over there and break her fucking neck. Bye."

CHAPTER FIFTEEN

ASSASSINATION AND IMMIGRATION

"…that the murder of John Kennedy is a straight mob hit. Jimmy Hoffa, Carlos Marcello, and Santo Trafficante, arrange and execute the murder."

Investigative reporter Dan Moldea, offering his opinion on the Kennedy assassination.

"'The mob did it. It's a historical fact."

Robert Blakey, chief counsel to the House Select Committee on Assassinations

Around the same time Sylvia attended Tony Pro's testimonial dinner in New Jersey, Robert Kennedy's justice department charged Jimmy Hoffa, Allen Dorfman, and five others with jury tampering in the Nashville case. A month later, Kennedy authorized another indictment charging Hoffa and seven other Teamsters for defrauding the Central States Pension Fund of over $20 million. But by the time the trials took place the following year, President John F. Kennedy, was dead.

Myriad volumes have parsed the evidence of a Mafia conspiracy in the Kennedy assasination, and Hoffa is linked in most accounts. Recall that in 1962—a year before the assasination—Teamsters snitch Edward Grady Partin had passed a lie detector test after telling investigators that Hoffa had told him of plans for a marksman to shoot Robert Kennedy while he rode in a covertabile in the South. In another alleged 1962 conversation, a Cuban refugee and CIA operative named Jose Aleman said that Santo Trafficante had told him that Kennedy was going to be "hit" and implied that Hoffa was involved in planning the crime. One of Hoffa's long-time lawyers, Frank Ragano, claimed that he had carried a message from Hoffa to Santo Trafficante and Carlos Marcello that ordered the crime of the century.

Kennedy's alleged killer, Lee Harvey Oswald, had ties to prime suspect and Hoffa ally Carlos Marcello. Oswald's killer, Jack Ruby, had ties to mobsters and unions in multiple cities, including Detroit, where Sylvia had met Ruby through the Laundry Workers Union and introduced him to Chuckie. Hoffa also knew Ruby from Detroit and Chicago, where Ruby was associated with Hoffa's close contact Red Dorfman. Both Oswald and Ruby had ties to Cuba. A series of phone calls between Ruby and close Hoffa aide Barney Baker in the days leading up to and following the assasination is often cited as another indication of Hoffa's involvement. In a report summarizing its lengthy congressional investigation of the assasination, the Church Committee determined that Jimmy Hoffa, Santo Trafficante and Carlos Marcello, had the means, motive, and opportunity to help kill the President.[18]

------

[18] Nevertheless, the Church Committee was unconvinced that Hoffa played a direct role in the crime. In the conclusion of their report, the Committee stated that it was, "improbable that Hoffa had anything to do with the death of the President."

Like Hoffa, Trafficante and Marcello were also under siege from the Kennedys' racket-busting efforts. Trafficante was further motivated by the Administration's Cuban policies and the impediments they placed on his ambitions to return to the island and reclaim his gambling empire. Marcello's motives were highly personal: In 1961, Robert Kennedy had orchestrated a surprise arrest in which Marcello was picked up off a New Orleans street, shoved onto a plane, and deported to the jungles of Guatemala with nothing but the clothes on his back.

The prevailing theory has the crime families believing that killing Bobby would be like cutting off the tail of a mighty and wrathful beast. Better to cut off the head by killing the President. The word on the streets was that the President's successor, Vice President Lyndon B. Johnson, hated Bobby Kennedy and would surely replace him as Attorney General, ending once and for all the younger Kennedy's assaults on the Teamsters and organized crime. "Bobby Kennedy's just another lawyer now," Hoffa was quoted as saying after he was seen in a restaurant celebrating the assassination.

The prediction came true when Robert Kennedy stepped down as Attorney General. But it was too late for Jimmy Hoffa, whose latest prosecutions were already under way when Kennedy resigned. Allen Dorfman was acquitted in the jury tampering case, but Hoffa was convicted and sentenced to eight years in federal prison. In a second case in Chicago, Hoffa was convicted of receiving kickbacks on pension fund loans and received an additional five years. In a recorded conversation between Sylvia and Allen Dorfman following the Chicago verdict, Dorfman told Sylvia that Hoffa should have stuck with making loans to mob-connected clients and avoided less formidable loan-seekers. "Hoffa wouldn't be in this trouble if he would have stayed away from the ten-cent moochers," Dorfman told Sylvia. "He never had any trouble when he was dealing in New York and Chicago."

While Hoffa remained out on appeal, The FBI contined their surveillence of Giaclaone's Home Juice Company and Sylvia's apartment. The microphones might have been illegal, but they were fruitful in fillling the gaps in the FBI's knowledge of LCN. In April 1963, agents listened as the Giacalone brothers discussed Sylvia's connections to Nick and Carl Civella in Kansas City. The Giacalones revealed that Detroit captain Anthony Zerilli had recently met with Nick Civella in Miami, where Zerilli and Civella discussed Sylvia Pagano and the role she played as their liaison with Hoffa. That same month, the FBI documented phone calls Sylvia made to the Kansas City office of Missouri Lieutenant Governor Hilary Bush, a machine politician from the Pendergast era who had represented defendants in the voting fraud trials stemming from the corrupt and bloody 1934 election in Kansas City.

These revelations led to increased communication between the Detroit and Kansas City FBI offices, and they heightened the Bureau's interest in the woman in the shadows of the Mafia-Teamsters alliance.

Agents looked for ways to pressure Sylvia into turning on her associates, but *Facci* was hardly a shrinking violet, and she had frustratingly few vulnerabilites. She had no criminal history, and investigators had been unable to tie her to the arson at her home. But just when it seemed that Sylvia was impenetrable, an agent in the Kansas City office noticed that Sylvia had the same name as her deceased sister.

Enter the Immigration and Naturalization Service, which opened an investigation of Sylvia in early 1964. When INS agents contacted Sylvia by telephone, she was indignant and refused to provide any information. It was another sign of her commitment to the code of silence: 'don't cooperate with authorities, even when you have nothing to hide.'

When the INS persisted, Tony Jack's lawyer, Lawrence Burns, set up a meeting in his office. Sylvia said nothing at the meeting, but she learned that agents suspected her of being an illegal immigrant who had stolen the identity of her sister, whose name Sylvia's parents had given her after their first daughter had died as an infant. "They know that you are an American citizen," fumed Tony Jack. "What the hell is this bullshit?"

On May 7[th,] 1964, Syliva flew back to Kansas City to gather documentation of her citizenship. She stayed with her mother at 609 Forest and interacted with various friends and acquaintances, including an unnamed informant[19] who reported to the FBI that Sylvia was in town complaining that the INS was trying to deport her. Sylvia obtained copies of her birth certificate, her baptismal record from Holy Rosary Church, report cards from KC public schools, and affidavits from people who swore that she was born in Kansas City. On May 15, 1964, Sylvia flew back to Detroit on TWA just in time to be with Josephine Hoffa while Josie underwent surgery.

The case stretched out for a full year, during which time INS and FBI agents documented Sylvia's mail. She received

---

[19] Possibly Joe Bates (codename "Root Beer"), a Teamster who married Charlie Binaggio's widow and served as a driver and close aide to Roy Williams.

frequent letters from Allen Dorfman's insurance companies in Chicago and packages from LaSalle Distributing, a Detroit retail goods outlet owned by Nathan Wygod, a high-rolling gambler who was later implicated in an interstate gambling conspiracy with high-ranking Chicago Outfit members Jackie Cerone and Donald "The Wizard of Odds" Angelini.

The threat of deportation to a country Sylvia had never set foot in would have been a strong bargaining chip for the FBI, but the lack of any evidence aside from her name indicates that the investigation was a merely a fishing expedition designed to gather more information on Sylvia and perhaps frustrate her into some level of cooperation. But the feds came up short; Sylvia said precisely nothing, and in December 1964, the INS tersely conceded that Sylvia was, "a native-born United States Citizen."

CHAPTER SIXTEEN

STEALING MONEY FROM HOFFA

"My mother taught me not to be a fool. She always taught me and taught me very well, schooled me, about both sides [the Teamsters and LCN]. 'Don't put yourself in a position to hurt either side.'"

Chuckie O'Brien

Hoffa's criminal convictions furthered his reputation as a villain, but a contemporaneous achievement made him more popular than ever with rank-and-file Teamsters. Four days before he went on trial for jury tampering, Hoffa signed the "National Master Freight Agreement," a uniform contract that standardized wages, working conditions and benefits for virtually all over-the-road truck drivers in North America. It was a historic accomplishment and Hoffa's finest hour as a labor leader. Even many of his critics conceded that he had secured a landmark triumph for laboring families. The union still trumpets the contract today as watershed moment in their history: "The NMFA of 1964 brought more workers into the middle class than any other single event in labor history," boasts the IBT website. The NMFA solidified Hoffa's support among the vast majority of Teamsters. "Hoffa may have been a crook," said a truck driver from Missouri, "but he made sure that the bottom man, the driver, got his cut. He worked for us."

Hoffa's contrasting images of hero and antihero made him a source of public fascination and kept him in the limelight while he remained free on appeal. He continued his marathon work schedule while Sylvia's son watched his back from a few steps away. In 1965, labor journalist Victor Riesel, whose eyesight Johnny Dio had destroyed with the acid attack a decade earlier, wrote that Chuckie O'Brien was Hoffa's, "intimate companion, driver, bodyguard and special troubleshooter."

Chuckie's troubleshooting duties included efforts to keep Hoffa out of prison. Edward Grady Partin, the turncoat Teamster who was the government's key witness in the jury tampering case and the source of Hoffa's alleged lone gunman plot that foreshadowed the Kennedy assassination, claimed that Chuckie O'Brien approached him during this time and offered him large sums of money for him to recant his testimony.

Sylvia continued to act as a liason to Hoffa and as an intermediary between other men in the Teamsters and the mob. FBI summaries of 1964 conversations captured on the hidden microphones show that Tony Jack used Sylvia to communicate with other powerful associates besides Hoffa: "ANTHONY GIACLAONE had stated to SYLVIA PARIS that the next time she was in contact with WILLIAM BUFALINO that she should mention to him that GEORGE RUBIN, who owns the Atlantic Towers Motel in Miami, Florida, was a friend of theirs and that BUFALINO should do something to assist him." Tony Jack also asked Sylvia to find a job for Tony "Shrieky" Thomas, a close Giacalone associate who was later found beaten to death in a dumpster in 1980.

But Sylvia was doing more than favors; she was also making deals and doing business with the boys. Through her association with Allen Dorfman's insurance companies, Sylvia had somehow gotten an insurance agent's license from the state of California and was now going into business with Dominic Licavoli. "I take 60 percent of the premiums and give her 40 percent," Licavoli told Tony Jack, who asked Sylvia if she could get a $400,000 life insurance policy for Mike Polizzi, the longtime Detroit *capo* with an accounting degree who had benefited from earlier pension fund loans brokered by Sylvia. Some of Sylvia's insurance business was tied to Hoffa and the Teamsters: "TONY talks about the insurance deal with SYLVIA saying that they have a $600,000 deal going and that they will get 10% of that. JIMMY HOFFA will get $30,000, SYLVIA will get $15,000, and they will have to divide the other $15,000 between them."

Recordings also reveal that Tony Jack used Sylvia as an intermediary between himself and his own money. The tapes demonstrate the high trust he placed in her, but also a willingness to expose Sylvia to prosecution. One transcript summary describes Giacalone's efforts to deposit large sums of illegal proceeds into various banks. In all such surveilliance reports, the FBI used the term "informant" as a euphamism for the illegal microphones: "Informant advised that TONY GIACALONE utilizes SYLVIA PARIS to handle some of the money and the fact is that she is to say, if she is ever questioned, that her husband left her $100,000 when he died. Informant advised that TONY GIACLAONE said he would definitley use SYLVIA PARIS if the government started investigating his income tax too thoroughly."

But money laundering wasn't the only crime that Giaclaone brought Sylvia into. He also enlisted her as an accomplice to theft—from none other than Jimmy Hoffa.

It was no secret that Hoffa kept absurd amounts of cash in safes at IBT Headquarters and in his residences in Detroit, Washington, and Miami. Much of the money came from kickbacks on pension fund loans and the Las Vegas skim. In early 1964, agents listened in as their "informant"—the illegal Home Juice bug—captured the Giacalones schemeing to get their hands on some of the money while Hoffa was tied up at trial in Tennessee:

> "Informant advised on January 15, 1964, that ANTHONY and BILLY GIACALONE were still considering the possibility of robbing the safe of JAMES R. HOFFA in Washington, D.C. and that they were considering going to Washington on January 23 or 24, 1964, while SYLVIA PARIS was still in Washington, D.C.
>
> According to the informant, they believed that this safe is located in a closet and it does not have a burglar alarm. They also believed that possibly the safe was made by JIMMY HOFFA himself.
>
> The informant stated that possibly after they had broken into it, he might think that JOSEPHINE HOFFA had gotten drunk and given the money away.
>
> The informant advised that ANTHONY GIACALONE had three sets of keys which were possibly to HOFFA'S apartment.

The informant stated that the GIACALONE boys, after they had robbed Hoffa's safe, planned on going right down to Florida under aliases in an attempt to throw people off the track. Informant stated that it was GIACALONE'S belief that HOFFA must have at least a half million dollars[20] in this safe.

Informant advised on 2/17/64 that the Subject attempted to contact SYLVIA PARIS in Wash. D.C. It is believed that PARIS is residing with JOSEPHINE HOFFA, the wife of JAMES HOFFA, at HOFFA'S Wash. apartment.

Informant advised on February 27, 1964, that Vito and Tony GIACALONE are still considering the possibility of burglarizing the safe in the apartment of James R. Hoffa in Washington, D.C.

It is believed the Subject will be in contact with SYLVIA PARIS while in Wash."

Agents watched as the Giaclaone brothers boarded a plane in Detroit and flew to Washington to carry out their plan, which called for Tony Jack to rob the safe while his brother and Josephine would "zoop it up" in the other room. Everything went according to plan unil the key they had made to open the safe didn't work. Tony Jack grabbed some cash that was lying outside the safe and made his exit.

The consolation cash wasn't enough to satisfy the Gaicalones' safecracking desires. They shifted their attention

---

[20] Over $5 million in 2026 dollars

to Miami, where Tony Jack had a tenth-floor apartment in a building adjacent to Hoffa's. According to Hoffa's lawyer Frank Ragano, "The rent for [Hoffa's] luxury three-bedroom penthouse was one dollar per year; a gratuity from the grateful developer of the building, who had been a recipient of a Fund loan."

While Sylvia and Josephine were out to dinner, Tony Jack gained access to Hoffa's safe but again failed to open it. He found some more consolation cash and took it, later telling his brother that he hoped Hoffa wouldn't notice the missing money for approximately two weeks.

The trascripts make it clear that Sylvia, despite her love for Hoffa, was in on the schemes. Sylvia's involvement demonstrates her heirarchy of loyalties. She was commited to Hoffa and the Teamsters, but her alliegience to Giacalone and the secret society she had grown up with in Kansas City was paramount. In making the decision to cooperate with Tony Jack and steal from Hoffa, Sylvia likely rationalized that she was getting the bad end of the bargain with Josephine, and that Hoffa had more cash than he knew what to do with. Money held little importance for Hoffa aside from a means to power. His family was set for life, and he was too busy working to spend much on his own modest material desires. What Giacalone planned to steal might have been seen by Sylvia as excess funds that Hoffa would never need and might not ever miss.

If so, she was right; Hoffa never did miss the money. "He would have flipped his fuckin' lid if he found out," said Chuckie, who decades later still felt disgusted and humiliated by the plots. "It was wrong and I told my mother to stop, that she was hurting me. She did it for Uncle Tony."

CHAPTER SEVENTEEN

HOFFA GOES TO PRISON

"I hope you never have to go to prison. It's hell on earth, only hell couldn't be this bad."

Jimmy Hoffa

At the 1966 Teamsters convention in Miami Beach, Hoffa sponsored a measure allowing him to retain the presidency and appoint a caretaker president while he was in prison. The delegates approved it, and Hoffa was reelected to a five-year term with a $25,000 increase in his salary.

When the Supreme Court turned down his appeal, Hoffa appointed his loyal underling Frank Fitzsimmons as acting President and gave Sylvia's friend Allen Dorfman complete control over the Central States Pension Fund.

On March 7, 1967, Chuckie O'Brien fought back tears as he prepared to drive Hoffa to the Department to Justice building where Hoffa would surrender to U.S. Marshals. "He didn't want to start the car," said Hoffa. "He was all broke up." Hoffa would loose more than a few allies while he was in prison, but Sylvia's son was a rock, visiting Hoffa regulary, starting a "Free Hoffa" campaign,[21] and remaining completely loyal to his "dad."

---

[21] Chuckie's campaign included the "Free Hoffa" bumper stickers that were ubiquitous on tractor-trailers in the 1960's and 70's.

Among Hoffa's fellow prisoners at the Lewisburg Federal Penitentiary in Pennsylvania were his old friend Tony Provenzano, who had been convicted of extorting a trucking company for labor peace, and Carmine Galante, the underboss of the Bonnano Family who was reported to have attended the 1957 Grand Hotel conclave in Sicily with Sylvia's old flame, Frank Coppola. Boston mobster Vincent Teresa said that Hoffa was one of the few men in the prison Galante would speak to.

Hoffa made an ally out of Carmine Galante, but an enemy out of Tony Provenzano during a fiery argument over $1 million in IBT compensation that Tony Pro felt he was due. Provenzano owed much to Hoffa, including his high-salaried position as an International Vice President, but Hoffa was finished doing favors for Pro and he told the gangster as much. It was the type of beef Sylvia could have helped mediate back home, but in prison it flared into a shoving match, and Sylvia's two close friends became bitter enemies.

While Hoffa stuffed mattresses in the prison workshop, Sylvia's close friend in Chicago, Allen Dorfman, lived in the lap of luxury as one of the nation's most powereful finaciers. According to Hoffa's lawyer Frank Ragano, Dorfman started gouging loanseekers after Hoffa went away. On July 28, 1967, Dorfman was exiting his driveway in a friend's Cadillac when the car was hit by three blasts from a shotgun. "If they had wanted to kill him they would have," Santo Trafficante told Ragano. "This was just a warning to get him to straighen out."

Frank Fitzsimmons didn't need a warning. The mob was entirely pleased with Hoffa's submissive interim president, who let them do pretty much whatever they wanted. Ulike

Hoffa, who couldn't be "bulldogged" and wasn't even afraid to go toe-to-toe with Tony Provenzano in prison, Fitzsimmons was a pushover. "Hoffa had always been a force in his own right," wrote investigative journalist Jonathan Kwitny. "He always required a favor for a favor granted. Fitzsimmons is a stooge, albeit a well-paid one. Sweetheart contracts can be signed and the union's treasury and pension fund can be raided free of potential interference. The Mafia chain of command can call the shots, as it prefers to do."

As Hoffa served his time, Fitzsimmons became more comfortable in the President's chair and more entrenched in his power. Loyalties and alliances were shifting away from Hoffa, and his power with the crime families was weakening. But Hoffa still had the unwavering support of the rank-and-file, and he fully intended on reclaiming his place at the top of the IBT when he got out of prison.

CHAPTER EIGHTEEN

SYLVIA'S DEATH

"God took her and it broke my heart. I know that she is in heaven and will help me as much as she did on earth."

Chuckie O'Brien

Hoffa's imprisonment marked a decline in Chuckie O'Brien's status and stability. Acute feelings of defeat corresponded with a downward spiral in other areas of Chuckie's life, including his marriage. One of the last things Hoffa did before going to prison was speak to Chuckie and Maryann about their problems. In his typically commanding style, he told his wingman and his daughter's best friend to "straighten things out."

Sylvia's relationship with Maryann had never been as harmonious as Chuckie might have imagined when he married a woman whose background and appearance reflected his mother. Sylvia and Maryann worked hard to coexist, and detente seemed to prevail in most of their interactions, but recordings reveal typical tensions between a wife and a mother-in-law who is heavily influential in her son's life. Sylvia is on tape crying during phone calls with Chuckie in which she complained of "mean" treatment by Maryann. To Tony Jack, Sylvia admonished Maryann's "sloppy" housekeeping, and habit of being "gone all day and playing cards all night." "SYLVIA says that she has been cow-towing to MARY ANN for 11 years," says an FBI summary of a recorded conversation. Another report documents Sylvia telling Tony Jack that Maryann could, "go back to Kansas City for all I care."

But statements uttered in emotional moments did not capture the complexity of Sylvia's relationship with her daughter-in-law. According to her grandson, Sylvia was furious when Chuckie told her he was going to divorce Maryann. "She told him to go back," said Chuck O'Brien.

By 1968 Chuckie was consumed with frustrations and anxieties that boiled over when he beat up a man whom he wrongly believed was having an affair with Maryann. It was the last straw for Maryann, and the couple divorced later that year.

Sylvia might have disapproved of Chuckie's divorce but she was still his harbor, especially with Hoffa away. Estranged from his wife and marginalized from his children, Chuckie needed his mother now more than ever.

And he had no reason to think she wouldn't be there for him. She was still relatively young and her health seemed fine. Her grit hadn't faded and she continued to "take care of everything" for her loved ones and the union and LCN associates who depended on her.

Sylvia also continued to travel frequently, especailly to Florida and New York, often in the company of her friend Ginger Blair, a Jewish woman from Detroit with cosmetics businesses in Miami and New Jersey who bore a resemblance to Sylvia and wore the same brunette bouffant. Coincidentally, she was married to an Italian named Luliano who went by the name of "Jack O'Brien."

In December 1970, Sylvia and Ginger met in Manhattan, where they were enjoying a Christmas-shopping trip when Sylvia was struck down by a massive heart attack. Sylvia was pronounced dead on December 17, 1970. She was 56 years-old.

For Chuckie, it was the worst thing that could possibly happen. Jack Goldsmith offered a succinct summary of the effect Sylvia's death had on his stepfather: "The loss hit him like nothing else ever had. Sylvia was his only close relative. He had always idolized her. She helped him out of his many scrapes, gave him money during his frequent pinches, and guided his major life choices…his main advisor, his champion, the person he knew had his back and guarded his interests, was gone."

"My dad was a mess," said Sylvia's grandson. "He was extremely upset, and the fact that her death was so unexpected made it that much worse. He was going through a lot of stuff workwise and family wise. When Nonna Sylvia died, it pulled the rug out from under him. I don't think he ever got over it."

Sylvia Pagano died in the metropolis where her mother had been born and where Pellegrino Scaglia began the chain of events that had helped shape her life and her destiny as the woman who introduced Jimmy Hoffa to *La Cosa Nostra* and facilitated the relations hip for 30 years. It goes without saying that the Mafia never inducted women into its ranks, but if they had, Sylvia Pagano would have been their first choice. They respected her, they profited from her, and she lived truer to the code than many of the men.

When Sylvia died, so too did Jimmy Hoffa's best chance to get back in the good graces of his old allies in the mob.

Sylvia's mosoleum at Holy Sepulchre Cemetery in the Detroit suburb of Southfield.

CHAPTER NINETEEN

POST PRISON POWER STRUGGLE

"Based on the above investigation, it is felt that Anthony and Vito Giacalone were acting in a capacity of mediators, to settle unknown differences between JRH and Anthony Provenzano."

FBI "Hoffex" memo

On December 23, 1971, less than five years into his 13-year sentence, Hoffa was released from prison when President Richard Nixon commuted his sentence to time served. Nixon solidified a Teamsters endorsement with the deal and also, according to rumors, a clandestine $1 million in campaign cash. Sylvia's son claimed to have delivered a breifcase full of cash provided by Frank Fitzsimmons to a man in a darkened room at the Madison Hotel in Washington, D.C. Chuckie believed the cash was Hoffa's own money, used to buy his freedom, but others claimed that Frank Fitzsimmons and Tony Provenzano had raised half the money and used it to buy an attachment to Hoffa's commutation that banned him from holding office in organized labor until 1980.

Hoffa saw the ban as the ultimate double cross by Fitzsimmons, and his former minion became his bitter enemy. Tony Provenzano could relate, and Fitz and Pro strengthened their alliance. Most other mafiosi still liked and respected Hoffa, but they were enjoying Fitz's gravy train. "Anything they wanted, they got," said Detroit organized crime investigator Vincent Piersante. While Hoffa was in prison, Fitz had given the mob almost unlimited access to the Fund and more control over locals and joint councils. Hoffa had always been a tougher nut to crack, and the mob's best controlling lever over him had died on a shopping trip to Manhattan. The Mafia did not respect Fitzsimmons like they did Hoffa, but they could control him.

The crime syndicate might have preferred Fitzsimmons, but Hoffa knew he had the overwhelming support of rank-and-file Teamsters. He began challenging the legality of Nixon's ban and speaking publicly about taking back leadership of the union. Hoffa's Sicilian associates told him to forget about it and enjoy his retirement, but Hoffa was obsessed with reclaiming what he thought of as his rightful place atop the IBT.

Just as it had been four decades earlier, Detroit's Local 299 was the starting point of Hoffa's path to victory. When Hoffa had resigned his presidency of Local 299 in advance of his commutation, the interim presidency had gone to Hoffa's ally and surrogate, Dave Johnson. "Everything hinged on his taking over Local 299," said Johnson. "Everything meant nothing if he couldn't do that."

Hoffa might have had an ally as Local 299 president, but the vice-presidency was held by Frank Fitzsimmons' son, Richard Fitzsimmons, who was challenging Dave Johnson for the presidency in the 1974 election. It was a make-or-break election for Hoffa, who would be shut out if Richard Fitzsimmons defeated Dave Johnson. The stakes were high, and Teamster violence flared again in Detroit.

In January, 1972, a bomb exploded at the home of a pro-Hoffa business agent named Gene Page. Six months later, another Hoffa loyalist named George Roxburgh lost his right eye after he was shotgunned while sitting in his Cadillac. Dave Johnson's office window was shot out and his 45-foot cabin cruiser was blown to smithereens by a bomb at the dock of his lakeside home. A pro-Fitzsimmons business agent named Ralph Proctor was beaten unconscious in a hotel parking lot. Hoffa ally Red Anderson's home was bombed. Other acts of violence in the power struggle included the burning of a Hoffa man's barn and the beating of a Teamster rebel by "three of Hoffa's goons," two of whom were later found murdered.

Defeating Fitzsimmons meant winning back the support of mafiosi who were prospering with Hoffa's rival. The alliance that Sylvia had forged decades earlier had served Hoffa well, but the mob now had enough power in the IBT to make or break his plans. "Because of the mob's tremendous influence in the Teamsters Union, Hoffa had no chance of returning to power unless the mob okayed it; that is a fact of life," said Detective Piersante.

Hoffa began setting up meetings with crime bosses only days after his release from prison. In Jauary, 1972, he met with Russell Bufalino in Miami. Hoffa had fallen out with Sylvia's friend, Bill Bufalino, while he was in prison, but he was still on good terms with his former lawyer's cousin, the Don of greater Pennsylvania. Russell Bufalino's right-hand man, Billy D'Elia, said that Russell loved Hoffa and quietly cautioned him to "go slow and not ruffle any feathers."

Another meeting in Miami was less amicable. A few months after meeting with Bufalino, Hoffa swallowed his pride and met with Tony Provenzano. Tony Giacalone arranged the meeting with his wife's cousin as a favor to his old friend and perhaps also to Sylvia, who would have wanted Tony Jack to make peace between her two dear friends. Hoffa, though, was hardly motivated by sentimentality; he needed the East Coast delegates that Provenzano still controlled for reelection. But prison tensions had not subsided, and the two hot-headed Teamsters came to blows after Tony Pro threatened Hoffa and his family if Hoffa didn't drop his bid to reclaim power. Before the meeting, a Miami Local 390 official named Lloyd Hicks had told friends that he was arranging to have the meeting secretly recorded. Hicks was found dead in the hours after the Hoffa-Provenzano meeting, shot 12 times. Some investigators specualted that Hick's murder was, at least in part, another warning sent to Hoffa from Provenzano. But Hoffa would not be cowed.

Sylvia's pal Allen Dorfman went to prison only two months after Hoffa was released. Dorfman had been convicted of taking a $55,000 kickback for arranging a $1.5 million loan to a wheeler-dealer named George Horvath. By Dorfman's own standards, it was a "ten-cent moocher" loan—the same type that he told Sylvia he blamed for Hoffa's indictment on similar charges. Dorfman was sentenced to one year and was out in 10 months on good behavior.

Dorfman's antithesis to a ten-cent moocher was Sylvia's other pal, Moe Dalitz. By the early 1970's, Dalitz had shifted his attention from Las Vegas to Carlsbad, California, where he and his partners built a Teamsters-financed country club and recreation spa called La Costa. The Dalitz group received 31 pension fund loans totaling $97 million[22] for the

---

[22] Approximately $750 million in 2026 dollars

project. La Costa soon became notorious as a spot where Teamsters and gangsters mixed with members of the Nixon Administration. Allen Dorfman and Frank Fitzsimmons had luxury condominiums adjacent to the golf course.

While Frank Fitzsimmons golfed at La Costa, Hoffa became emboldened by a survey that showed 83 percent of dues-paying Teamsters supporting Hoffa over Fitzsimmons were the two to challenge each other in the 1976 election. Hoffa's parole was also ending, and his legal challenges to the ban prohibiting him from union activity until 1980 were looking promising. With these winds at his back, Hoffa decided to go public with his grievances against Fitzsimmons and his intentions to take back the Teamsters. He began giving interviews and started writing a book. He even spoke publicly about ridding the organized crime element from the union and the pension fund.

It fell to Tony Jack to fix the Hoffa problem. As Hoffa's early LCN contact, Mafia protocol gave Giacalone a large degree of jurisdiction and responsibility over Hoffa. Thanks to Sylvia, Hoffa had been both a gold mine and a source of high status for Giacalone. If Hoffa took back the Teamsters with Giacalone's help, Tony Jack could expect to prosper accordingly. Giacalone liked and respected Hoffa, and both men were bonded by Sylvia and Chuckie. Even while Tony Pro was itching to kill Hoffa, Tony Jack worked to smooth things over and make peace. But Hoffa was obstinate. He balked at meeting with Tony Pro, and Giacalone watched the ice getting thiner under Hoffa's feet. Chuckie was caught in the emotional pull of one uncle trying to stave off the execution of a father by another uncle. If only his mother were alive. If anyone could save Hoffa from Provenzano—and save him from himself—it was Sylvia.

But to Chuckie's dismay, his mother was dead. His pain over Sylvia's death was still raw when, two years later, he lost his grandmother. Sylvia's mother, Maggie Campo Pagano, was 81 years-old and still living at 609 Forest in KC's Little Italy when she died. Chuckie had spent almost as much of his youth with her as he had with his own mother, and his own children had visited her regularly along with their other grandparents on trips from Detroit. Chuckie's divorce had alienated him from his own children and made him less welcome in Kansas City. And things were no better in Detroit, where Chuckie's relationship with the only father he had ever known was fracturing in the midst of the Teamsters power struggle.

These were dark days for Sylvia's son, but Chuckie's confidence in his mother to "help me as much as she did on earth" was rewarded with a phone call from a woman Sylvia had introduced him to years earlier. Brenda Berger was the Arkansas beauty queen daughter of one of Sylvia's best friends, a similarly gritty Southern woman named Clemmye whom Sylvia met on one of her frequent trips to Miami. Brenda was Chuckie's lifeline to a new family and a new life in Florida, where Chuckie would become a model stepfather to Brenda's three sons, including his future biographer, Jack Goldsmith. Chuckie's relationship with Brenda would last the rest of his life, but their honeymoon was barely over when Chuckie's new family would find themselves drawn into one of the crimes of the century.

With Sylvia gone, the person most likely to talk sense into Jimmy Hoffa seemed to be Russell Bufalino, who sat down with Hoffa again on October 18, 1974 in Philadelphia at a meeting that included Philly boss Angelo Bruno and Bufalino's wingman, Billy D'Elia, who said that Bufalino told Hoffa that he was in danger if he didn't stop doing what he was doing and saying what he was saying. Hoffa responded, "Russell, you're my friend and with all respect…I built that fucking union from nothing. I have to do what I have to do and I'm getting my union back."

Bufalino sadly washed his hands of Hoffa, but Tony Giacalone kept trying. His persistence was almost certainly influenced by Sylvia in a mix of loyalty, nostalgia, and frustration at the fact that his old flame wasn't there to talk sense into Jimmy Hoffa. Asking Chuckie to intervene was unfortunatly out of the question. In Hoffa's eyes, O'Brien had joined the ranks of defectors who had betrayed him for Fitzsimmons. "[O'Brien] was told by Fitzsimmons that he was going to be sent to Alaska," said Hoffa. "Word filtered down to me that O'Brien "made peace" with Fitzsimmons and was to get, instead of the freeze-out, a plush assignment to Florida. Proving, I guess, that self-preservation really is the first law of nature no matter what they say about biting the hand that feeds you."

But Hoffa wasn't feeding Chuckie anymore; Fitzsimmons was, and Fitz had made it clear that Chuckie's job was on the line if he stayed in Hoffa's camp. Chuckie could hardly be blamed for clinging to his livelihood, especially after Hoffa failed to keep a promise he had made to reward Chuckie's loyalty by backing him for the presidency of Local 299. Chuckie was also questioning Hoffa's sanity in speaking publicly about exposing mob influence in the Teamsters—effectively threatening to become a rat. "You're putting a bonfire under me," Chuckie told Hoffa. "You know where I came from. You knew who my mother was. You know I'm from Kansas City."

Chuckie knew that Kansas City was not happy with Hoffa. "I used to talk to Willie [Cammisano] about it," Chuckie said. "It's not good, Chuckie, it's not good," said Cammisano.

With Sylvia's son neutralized, Giacalone thought that maybe her old friend Moe Dalitz could straighten Hoffa out. He set up a meeting in Las Vegas.

On June 9, 1975, Hoffa and Vito Giacalone met with Moe Dalitz, Morris Shenker, and Chicago Outfit heavy Joey "The Clown" Lombardo at the Dunes Hotel and Casino. Thirty years had passed since Sylvia introduced Hoffa to Dalitz. During that time, they made millions together and built Las Vegas into an international destination. But not even Moe Dalitz could convince Hoffa to bow out. It would be Hoffa's last trip to the city where once he was Ceasar.

With a level of patience more characteristic of Sylvia than the street boss of Detroit, Tony Jack arranged yet another meeting on Hoffa's behalf, this time with the godfather Sylvia had known the longest: Nick Civella. Civella had gotten closer to Sylvia's friend, Allen Dorfman, in recent years, and Dorfman had recently approved a $62.7 million[23] loan to Civella's frontman, Allen Glick, for the purchase of the Stardust and Freemont casinos in Las Vegas. Civella was also jockeying for his man Roy Williams to succeed Frank

---

[23] Approximately $430 million in 2026 dollars.

Fitzsimmons as IBT President. Hoffa and Civella were old friends, but Civella's plans did not include Hoffa, and Hoffa's entreaties were met by a stern rebuke from the Kansas City boss.

Giacalone had run out of options. None of Sylvia's old friends had been able to reason with him as she might have been able to. Hoffa's meeting with Civella ended once and for all his chances of clawing back underworld support from Fitzsimmons. Giacalone had kept Hoffa alive for at least a year longer than Provenzano and others would have liked, but after Hoffa's meeting with Civella, Giacalone could no longer fight the current.

If there were any remnants of hope that Hoffa would get wise and retire, they were blown sky high on July 10, 1975, when Richard Fitzsimmons narrowly escaped death as he exited Nemo's Bar & Grille in Detroit. "I got up to leave and was on my way to my car when I saw it explode," said the younger Fitzsimmons. The brand new Lincoln Continental given to Fitzsimmons by Local 299 burned in a mass of mangled metal, and all eyes looked to Jimmy Hoffa.

Two days later, the Giacalone brothers met with Hoffa at the lake house and again implored him to meet with Provenzano. They explained that Tony Pro would be in Detroit later that month for the wedding of Bill Bufalino's daughter. Other leading mafiosi from around the country would also be attending, and it would be the perfect time for Hoffa to settle the beef. Hoffa seemed to recognize that Giacalone had gone above and beyond to help him, and he finally agreed to the meeting. But Hoffa did not realize that Tony Jack's assistance had already ended, and that Giacalone was now luring Hoffa to his death.

Sylvia's sweetheart, Anthony "Tony Jack" Giacalone, six weeks before Hoffa's disappearance.

CHAPTER TWENTY

DISAPPEARANCE

"It appears from all investigation to date, that O'Brien was used as an instrument by Tony Giacalone in the disappearance of JRH. O'Brien is known to be one of the few persons JRH would get into a car with."

FBI "Hoffex" memo, 1975

Tony Pro was merely the bait. On July 30th 1975, the day of Hoffa's disappearance, Provenzano would be nowhere near Detroit. With his alibi firmly established at a card game at the Local 560 union hall in Union City, New Jersey, Hoffa's enemy awaited news from the henchmen he had sent to Detroit to assist with the plan.

Giacalone arranged with Hoffa to meet at the Machus Red Fox restaurant in Bloomfield Township. But when a maroon-colored sedan arrived at the Red Fox to pick up Hoffa, Giacalone was at the Southfield Athletic Club, enjoying a leisurely day that included a haircut and manicure while solidifying his alibi by ostentasiously asking other members what time it was.

Investigators have long debated who exactly was in that car, but they've all agreed that Hoffa would not have gotten in unless he trusted the occupants. And who among Giaclaone's close associates would Hoffa trust with his life? Sylvia's son, of course.

Or would he? Was Hoffa's anger at Chuckie enough to repell him, or was it transcended by a lifetime of loyalty and trust? Investigators believed it was the latter, and Chuckie's actions on the day of Hoffa's dissapearance provided agents with reasonable suspicion that Sylvia's son had—either knowingly or unkowingly— driven Hoffa to his death. In the days following the disappearance, Hoffa's surrogate son became the leading suspect, and he would remain so for decades.

On the morning of July 30th, a friend dropped O'Brien off at Local 299 Headquarters. Around 12:00 p.m., Chuckie borrowed a 1975 maroon-colored Mercury Marquis from Tony Jack's son, Joseph "Joey Jack" Giacalone. While Chuckie used the car to run a series of errands, Hoffa left home for his 2:00 p.m. meeting with Giacalone and Provenzano. He told Josephine he would be back by 4:00 p.m. to grill her a steak dinner.

At the Machus Red Fox, the puctuality-obsessed Hoffa spoke to several people who recognized him and later described him as looking impatient for whomever he was waiting for.

At 2:45 p.m., a witness saw Hoffa getting into a maroon-colored car matching the description of Joey Jack's Mercury Marquis with three other men. The witness's description of the driver matched the physical appearance of Chuckie O'Brien.

At 4:30 p.m., FBI agents conducting routine surveillance watched Detroit underboss Giacomo "Black Jack" Tocco enter the Southfield Athletic Club and meet with Tony Jack behind closed doors. Billy Jack followed Black Jack and met with Tony Jack an hour later for a casual dinner at their favorite table at the club's grille.

Hoffa's car was located in the Red Fox parking lot early the next morning. His registered firearm was inside the car, but 62-year-old Jimmy Hoffa was missing, never to be seen again. Also in the parking lot that morning, waiting for a ride to work at Local 299, was Chuckie O'Brien. Chuckie claimed to have not yet been aware of Hoffa's disappearance, or to have noticed Hoffa's car, but his presence at the scene of the crime raised the eyebrows of investigators.

A day later, the Detroit Family hosted Teamster and Mafia royalty at the elegant wedding of Bill Bufalino's daughter at the lawyer's lavish estate in Grosse Pointe Shores. It was the event of the season, and not even a beaming Tony Provenzano could stay away. News of Hoffa's disappearance had already broke, but nobody at the wedding knew nothin'.

One of the first people to supect Chuckie was Jimmy Hoffa Junior, whose view of Chuckie had evolved from fun-loving big brother to wary rival. At a press conference days after the disappearance, Hoffa Jr. stopped short of accusing Chuckie of direct involvement, but insisted that Chuckie had knowledge of what had happened and was being evasive about his whearabouts on the day of the dissapearance. Hoffa Jr. also told detectives that Chuckie was one of the few people his father would've gotten into a car with.

Other sources implied that Chuckie had motive in the crime. High-ranking Teamster Jackie Presser told the FBI that Hoffa had promised to reward Chuckie's loyalty after he got out of prison by supporting Chuckie for elected office at Local 299, but failed to keep his promise. "As a result of all this,

Chuckie was very bitter to Jimmy Hoffa," said Presser, who also claimed that Chuckie helped fan the flames of Hoffa's demise: "By the Spring of '75, Chuckie hated Hoffa and his son so much that he was spreading word to the Outfit people that Jimmy Hoffa was talking to the FBI."

Others believed that Chuckie was involved, but only as an unwitting accomplice who did not know that he was chauffeuring Hoffa to his death. Hoffa's lawyer, Frank Ragano, reported what he claimed Santo Trafficante told him about the disappearance: "Tony Pro said that Tony Jack would have to get Chuckie to set Hoffa up because he trusted Chuckie and would go with him. That was the only way they thought they could get to Hoffa. Tony Jack didn't want to get Chuckie involved. He told Tony Pro that Chuckie is like family to him, like his nephew. He couldn't let anything happen to him. Tony Pro said, 'If you give me your word that Chuckie won't talk, then nothing will happen to him.' Tony Jack gave his word of honor that Chuckie would keep quiet after they took care of Hoffa…Poor Chuckie; they used him. He didn't know what was going on."

Chuckie became the leading suspect after a police dog detected Hoffa's scent in the back seat of Joey Giaclaone's Mercury, which officers had seized as evidence a few days after the disappearance. Agents also found a three-inch strand of hair in the car that was similar to samples taken from Hoffa's hairbrush.

Sylvia's son, Chuckie O'Brien, shortly after Hoffa's disappearance.

Chuckie did himself no favors when he spoke to the FBI and the media about the case, giving inconsistent accounts of his movements on the day of the disappearance and invoking his Fifth Ammendement rights before a federal grand jury that was investigating the crime. "O'BRIEN'S two FBI interviews are repleat with inconsistencies and untruths which collaterall interviews have proved," stated an FBI memo.

The FBI doubted that Chuckie had knowingly driven Hoffa to his death, but strongly suspected that he had done so unknowingly and was covering for his friends who had killed his hero.

Could Sylvia have saved Hoffa?

"My mother could get Hoffa to do anything the Outfit wanted."

But could she have done what Tony Jack couldn't: get Hoffa to clear the air with Provenzano and abandon his plans to take back the union? Or could she have provided the level of control over Hoffa that would have made his presidency more palatable to the Mafia? Considering Hoffa's obstinance and the Syndicate's preference for Fitzsimmons, probably not.

But like Sylvia's grandson said, "If anyone could have saved Jimmy Hoffa, it would've been her."

EPILOGUE

"My father hated rats. But he was a sweet man; very kind, very generous. Too generous, really. He would help anybody. He had a great sense of humor and he liked to cook for people. Everyone who knew him liked him. He became a godly man late in life, watching mass on TV and collecting holy cards."

Sylvia's grandson, Chuck O'Brien

Jimmy Hoffa's death remains one of the great unsolved mysteries in American history, but a degree of consensus exists among knowledgable investigators on what they see as a probable scenario:

One of the possible occupants of the sedan that drove Hoffa to his death was Salvatore "Sally Bugs" Briguglio, one of the underlings Tony Provenzano had sent from New Jersey. Hoffa would've recognized Sally Bugs as Tony Pro's guy, and his presence would have indicated that Hoffa was indeed on his way to meet Provenzano.

After leaving the parking lot of the Machus Red Fox restaurant, Hoffa was transported somewhere nearby and familiar. A house only three and a half miles from the Red Fox was owned by Carlo Licata, who had joined the Detroit Family after relocating from Los Angeles, where he had soldiered for Frank DeSimone, the Southern California boss whose father had long ago chosen to migrate to L.A. instead of Kansas City in the wake of the Pelligrino Scaglia killing in Pueblo. Licata had planted his flag in Detroit by marring the sister of Black

Jack Tocco. According to Scott Burnstein, author of *Motor City Mafia*, Hoffa had previously met Outfit members in Licata's home, so the location would not have raised alarms.

Vito "Billy Jack" Giacalone, who had had an affair with Hoffa's wife a decade earlier, is seen as another likely occupant of the sedan. Billy Jack's young soldier Tony Palazzolo has also been credibly implicated in the murder and seems to be the one most likely to have killed Hoffa, probably by strangulation.

According to Scott Burnstein, Sylvia's granddaughter's godfather, Vince Meli, "played a major role" in the conspiracy to murder Jimmy Hoffa. Meli had dined with Hoffa the night before the disappearance, and he later became the primary suspect in the "follow-up" murders of two Hoffa loyalists. Meli's uncle, Angelo Meli, had sat with Hoffa along with Sylvia's boyfriend, Frank Coppola, and Santo Perrone at the original meeting that Sylvia had brokered back in 1941.

But what happened to Hoffa's remains? Decades of rumors have led to suspenseful excavations at various sites, including a Provenzano-connected New Jersey landfill that Hoffa investigator Dan Moldea still believes to be Hoffa's final resting place. But others have a hard time imagining the Detroit Outfit taking the chance of transporting the dead body of anyone, let alone Jimmy Hoffa, across state lines, especially when they had the perfect place just a short distance from the Licata home. Central Sanitation, a trash processing company owned by Jimmy Quasarano and Pete Vitale, was equipped with an industrial incenerator capable of transforming teeth and bones into ashes. Much to the chagrin of true crime buffs who long for a resolution to the case, the remains of Jimmy Hoffa likely went up in smoke only a couple of hours after he was last seen leaving the parking lot of the Machus Red Fox restaruant. Arsonists torched Central Sanitation only a few months after Hoffa's disappearance.

The consensus is that Hoffa was killed to keep Fitzsimmons in power and prevent Hoffa from making good on his threats to rid the mob from the union. But informed sources also point to a secondary motive: the Church Committee and its investigation of the Kennedy assasinations and the CIA/Mafia plots to kill Fidel Castro. Three star witnesses, Sam Giancana, Jimmy Hoffa, and Johnny Roselli, were all murdered in advance of scheduled apperances to testify before the Committee. Giancana, the boss of the Chicago Outfit, was shot and killed only 6 weeks before Hoffa disappeared while cooking sausages in the basement of his home. Roselli, a dashing and well-traveled mobster who had represented Chicago's interests in California and Las Vegas, disappeared one year after Hoffa. His torso was found 10 days later stuffed into a 50 gallon drum floating in Florida's Dumfoundling Bay.

In the wake of Hoffa's death, the power base of the Mafia-Teamsters alliance that Sylvia had facilitated shifted from Detroit to her hometown of Kansas City, from where Nick Civella and Roy Williams called the shots, approved the loans, and enforced the discipline. Jackie Presser, the FBI informant who would later succeed Roy Williams as IBT President, offered several examples of KC's ascendency:

In April 1977, Presser reported that Frank Fitzsimmons had refused to renew Allen Dorfman's insurance contract with the Central States Conference of Teamsters. Dorfman got ahold of Nick Civella, who contacted Roy Williams and Tony Provenzano, who pressured Fitz into renewing Dorfman's contract. Presser also told the FBI that

Allen Dorfman and Nick Civella put a contract out on Dan Shannon, the director of the Central States Pension Fund, because Shannon was resisting Dorfman's loan requests.

In 1979, Civella hosted a midnight "sit-down" with Allen Dorfman and Roy Williams to mediate a dispute over a loan to Hoffa's former lawyer and Dunes Hotel and Casino owner, Morris Shenker. "In this instance Williams, an IBT vice president and a fiduciary for the union, had to appeal a union decision to the La Cosa Nostra crime boss of Kansas City," marveled a congressional committee.

By 1980, Jackie Presser called Nick Civella, "the single strongest Mafia voice in the union." In 1981, after Frank Fitzsimmons died of lung cancer, Civella convinced Fat Tony Salerno in New York and the families in Chicago and Cleveland to support his man Roy Williams for IBT President. The mob-controlled delegates delivered the election to Williams and handed Nick Civella a triumph that was a quarter-century in the making. "When Roy Lee Williams is given the mantle of power this week as president of the Teamsters Union, Nick Civella's crime family will rise to new heights of power in the ranks of organized crime nationally," wrote Kansas City labor columnist Michael Yablonsky.

Sylvia's family tree also shifted back to Kansas City. "My mom took me and my sister to Kansas City every summer when we were growing up," said Sylvia's grandson, Chuck O'Brien. "I actually had more friends in KC than I did in Detroit. Guys from Northeast and up North and from running around with my cousins and playing baseball and tackle football at the Concourse. When I found out KC was getting a hockey team, that was it."

A diehard hockey fan since his days living on the same block with Gordie Howe and attending Red Wings games with his father, Sylvia's grandson had mastered the sport and played Division 2 at Hillsdale College. When the NHL announced that professional hockey was coming to Kansas City, O'Brien landed a job in public relations with the Kansas City Scouts.

Chuck arrived in Kansas City in a green 1971 Mustang that Sylvia had bought for him as a high school graduation gift shortly before she died. "I never knew she paid for it. I thought my dad did until he told me the story later on. I wish I could have thanked her for it. I wish she would have lived longer."

Before starting his job with the NHL, Chuck worked a short stint at the Godfather Lounge, an establishment owned by one of his uncles that was located in the River Quay, the northside nightlife district that would soon explode into a phantasmagoric scene of bombings, shootings, and arsons that would define the Mafia to a generation of Kansas Citians. "The FBI came to talk to me at my uncle's bar in '75 after Uncle Jimmy disappeared," said O'Brien. "I didn't know nothin' from nothin.' I said, 'I'm not talking to those guys.' But they kept coming around and finally I talked to them, but I didn't tell them anything because I didn't know anything. And quite frankly, if I did know anything, I wouldn't say anything anyway."

Two years after Chuck poured his last drink at the Godfather Lounge, the business was torched in the River Quay war. By then Chuck was living his dream working in professional hockey. Unfortunately for O'Brien, the Scouts only lasted two years in KC, and he wasn't interested in moving to Denver with the team. In a serendipitous career move, Chuck took up truck driving and spent the next 26 years with

Consolidated Freight and Local 41 of the Teamsters Union. He married an Italian girl from the old neighborhood and raised his family in Kansas City. He named his son Charles after himself, his father, his father's father, and a long line of previous Charles's that stretched all the way back to Ireland. Sylvia's great-grandson Charles has since had his own son, who is also named Charles.

Sylvia's granddaughter also left Detroit for Kansas City, where she married Willie Cammisano's son, Jerry Cammisano. It was a match that would seem to have pleased Sylvia, whose acquaintanceship with the Cammisanos went back to her youth in the North End. Sylvia might also have smiled on her granddaughter raising her own family in the Northland home that had once belonged to Sylvia's old friend, Nick Civella. Sylvia's great-grandson, Vito Cammisano, later became a bit of celebrity when he dated MU defensive lineman Michael Sam, the first openly gay player to be drafted in the NFL.

Sylvia's granddaughter was named after Josephine Hoffa.

***

On March 21, 1978, Salvatore "Sally Bugs" Briguglio was shot and killed on Mulberry Street in Manhattan's Little Italy. To most appearances, it was a case of Tony Provenzano eliminating any chance that Briguglio would talk about the Hoffa case. "When he heard of Briguglio's murder, Chuck O"Brien probably worried a little more," wrote Dan Moldea.

But Chuckie had other worries besides getting whacked. Lacking enough evidence to indict him in the Hoffa case, the government went after him on bribery and fraud charges. In 1978, chuckie was convicted of accepting a gift from a company whose workers he represented, and for misrepresenting his income on a bank loan application. The feds had hoped the charges would pressure Chuckie into cooperating in the Hoffa investigation, but Sylvia's son served his time and kept his mouth shut.

Shortly before Jimmy Hoffa disappeared, Sylvia's friend and business associate, Allen Dorfman, was indicted along with fellow Chicagoans Irwin Weiner, Joey "The Clown" Lomardo, and Tony "The Ant" Spilotro, for defrauding the pension fund of $1.4 million. The defendants beat the charges after the chief government wintess, Daniel Seifert, was shot and killed in Chicago.

On March 25, 1979, Dorfman and Joey the Clown flew to Kansas City for a meeting with Nick Civella. Surveilling agents in Chicago tipped off KC Agent Bill Ousley, who followed Dorfman and Lombardo to the Crown Center Hotel. Ousely managed to rent the room adjacent to the confab and press his ear to the connecting door. He heard Allen Dorfman beseeching Civella to ask Roy Williams to pressure Fitzsimmons into firing two asset management companies that had been assigned to the Central States Pension Fund under pressure from the government. Other highly sensitive business was discussed, and Agent Ousley took copious notes that fattened the files of the Strawman investigation, a historic case that brought down the Las Vegas skim; ensnared the leadership of the families in Kansas City, Chicago, Cleveland, and Milwaukee; and inspired Martin Scorcese's cinematic triumph, *Casino*.

Since Hoffa's death, Sylvia's two old friends, Allen Dorfman and Nick Civella, had worked together to maintain the Mafia's influence in the Teamsters Union. By then, Dorfman had presided over loans to organized crime operatives estimated at more than $500 million.[24] To Nick Civella, Dorfman was almost as valuable as Roy Williams, but unfortunately for Civella, both Dorfman and Williams were convicted in 1982 for conspiring to bribe U.S. Senator Howard Cannon to block a trucking deregulation bill. Dorfman was also facing other charges in Chicago and San Francisco. He was looking at up to 20 years in prison, and the mob feared he might make a deal with the government.

At high noon on Thursday, Jan. 20, 1983, Dorfman and Irwin Weiner were walking through the parking lot of the Hyatt House Hotel in Chicago. As they passed between two parked cars, killers snuck up from behind and put 7 bullets into Dorfman's head.

---

[24] Approximately $3 billion in 2026 dollars

On the sixth anniversary of Hoffa's disappearance, and inside the same home where Hoffa is thought to have been killed, Carlo Licata died with two gunshot wounds to the chest. His wife, Josephine Tocco, slept through the shooting. Licata's death was investigated as a possible suicide, but the pistol was found ten feet from Licata's body, and Licata's prints were not found on the gun. As in the cases of Sally Bugs and Allen Dorfman, no one was ever charged.

In October 1983, the widow of Pellegrino Scaglia died in Kansas City. Born in Pueblo 85 years earlier, Maria Scaglia's life had spanned the era of horse-drawn grocery wagons to the modern suburb of Overland Park, where she lived out her later years at 8101 Santa Fe Drive. It had been 60 years since the migration from Pueblo. Her husband's murder was a distant memory and a secret seldom spoken,[25] but through the niece of his brother, the murder of Pellegrino Scaglia and the subsequent diaspora to Kansas City reverberated all the way to the White House, touching the lives and affecting the fortunes and misfortunes of millions of ordinary Americans along the way.

As for the mafiosi who had remained in Pueblo, they continued their operations under the leadership of Vincenzo, "Black Jim" Colletti. The Family was remote, isolated, and off the radar, but in 1970, Detroit's Joe Zerilli, clad in a light blue summer suit and carrying a briefcase, was seen entering Colletti's modest home in Pueblo along with the skipper of New York's Genovese family, Gerardo Catena; Gambino family captain Joseph Riccobono; and an international gambler

---

[25] "It has always been my understanding he died of pneumonia," said Pellegrino's son, Missouri State Representative Phil Scaglia, to the FBI in the 1963.

with close ties to Meyer Lansky named John Pullman. Colletti seemed to be upping his family's game, but two days before Jimmy Hoffa disappeared, Colletti died at age 78, and the Pueblo Family began to fade into obscurity.

In 1979, Tony Giaclaone began serving a 10-year sentence for tax evasion and extortion. Giacalone was paroled after seven years and resumed his spot at the top of the Detroit Outfit. Giacalone remained very close to Chuckie and his family, hosting them often at his Florida residence and serving as an uncle to Chuckie's stepsons. He died on February 23, 2001, while under indictment in a sprawling federal racketeering case that spanned 30 years of criminal activity and included charges of infiltrating the Frontier and Aladdin casinos in Las Vegas—endeavors begun decades earlier with a $10 million pension fund loan obtained with Syliva's assistance.

A few months after his Uncle Tony died, a grieving Chuckie faced renewed scrutiny as the leading suspect in Hoffa's disappearance when the three-inch hair recovered 26 years earlier from Joey Giacalone's maroon-colored Mercury Marquis was put through DNA testing. The result: a dead ringer for Jimmy Hoffa. It seemed to show that Hoffa had indeed been in the car that Chuckie admitted to driving that very day. It did nothing to prove Chuckie's guilt, but it reinforced it in the minds of millions. Chuckie had never lived down the accusations, and now it looked like he never would.

As the leading suspect in one of the crimes of the century, Chuckie had spent decades living under the burdens of infamy and humiliation. The conventional wisdom was that he had either knowingly or unknowingly driven his surrogate father to his death. Chuckie was either ridiculed as a dupe or reviled as a perpetrator of patricide. It was not until 2019, when his stepson Jack Goldsmith's book, *In Hoffa's Shadow*, was released, that Chuckie was publicly humanized and vindicated in the Hoffa disappearance. A panel of FBI agents and Department of Justice lawyers corroborated Goldsmith's exoneration of his stepfather and finally cleared O'Brien as a suspect. One agent, Andrew Sluss, even stated, "It is a physical impossibility that Mr. O'Brien was with Hoffa when he disappeared."

But just when Chuckie's innocence seemed assured, a former *Detroit Free Press* reporter named Jo Thomas released her memoir, which included a chapter on Chuckie O'Brien and a strange encounter the reporter had with Chuckie on the very night that Hoffa disappeared. "Until I read a well-researched and sympathetic book written many years later by O'Brien's stepson, I do not realize O'Brien has misled his family and investigators about several critical things," said Thomas, who explained that Chuckie knew about Hoffa's disappearance earlier than he later claimed. "Chuckie tells me Jimmy is missing, and the Hoffa family is upset. But they have not spoken to him yet. So how does he know Hoffa has disappeared? And why, if he is not involved, does he lie afterward about when he knew?"

But these inconsistencies do not prove that Chuckie participated in the crime, and along with Goldsmith's evidence that he did not is the commonsense conclusion that if Chuckie really had driven Hoffa to his death—knowingly or not—he would have met the same fate as Sally Bugs and Carlo Licata. "If my dad was there, they would've killed him; it's that simple," said Sylvia's grandson. Frank Ragano's claim that Tony Giacalone guaranteed Chuckie's silence to Tony Provenzano in advance of the crime seems unrealistic, even naïve in the amount of compassion and trust that the ruthless Giacalone supposedly extended to Chuckie.

But what if it was true? Could Giacalone's love for Sylvia and his soft spot for her son have kept Chuckie alive? Even if Chuckie had not driven Hoffa on the fateful day, the pressure he was under as the leading suspect would ordinarily have made him a marked man. Chuckie knew plenty of incriminating information. Why take any chances that he might let something slip under intense questioning? Dan Moldea wrote that Chuckie was, "thought to be the only person who could finger Hoffa's killers without directly incriminating himself." This alone would've made Chuckie a liability, especially after he was indicted in 1978 on charges of labor extortion and bank fraud. Everyone understood that the government would offer him leniency in exchange for cooperation.

And yet Chuckie lived on. If voices in Detroit or beyond called for his execution, Giacalone forbade it. Uncle Tony's loyalty to Sylvia and fondness for her son seems to have included an ironclad trust in Chuckie as a "stand-up guy."

If so, Giacalone was right. The half-Irish kid from Kansas City proved to be the ultimate adherent to the code of *Omerta*. He withstood years of intense pressure from the government and did time in prison rather than turn on his associates. His silence cost him his reputation and, ultimately, his career, but even while dozens of hardened mafiosi betrayed the code, Sylvia Pagano's son kept quiet. "Uncle Tony would believe in me and my trust because he knew how my mother raised me," said Chuckie. "I would never rat anybody out, period. I just wouldn't do it…there's a code of honor…I would never betray Tony Giacalone. Never."

Like Frank Ragano and others,[26] the financially strapped Chuckie could have made good money with a tell-all book in his later years after the danger of reprisal had passed. But when Chuckie's stepson encountered frustrating refusals to reveal certain information about the Hoffa disappearance and people who had been dead for decades, he realized that Chuckie's vow of secrecy extended beyond the grave.

From beyond her own grave, Sylvia could look down with pride at her only child. Before Chuckie took his secrets to his own grave on February 13, 2020 at age 86 in Boca Raton, Florida, he told his stepson that whenever he was tempted to tell a secret that would help explain something—even if it would help to vindicate him—he would see Sylvia standing in front of him, reminding him of the code of silence.

---

[26] Frank "The Irishman" Sheeren wrote a bestselling but widely discredited account in which he claimed to have killed Hoffa. The book was made into the blockbuster film, *The Irishman*.

ADDENDUM

The International Brotherhood of Teamsters reached peaked membership under Jimmy Hoffa's leadership and began shrinking almost to the moment he stepped down as IBT President. IBT attrition has continued, but organized crime influence has also waned, and the union is no longer the bastion of corruption and violence it was in the 20th Century. The following testimonials offer a look into the post-Hoffa IBT and the experiences of two rank-and-file members of Kansas City's Local 41.

James Willis was born October 29, 1952 and grew up at 803 Pacific, just 7 blocks from Sylvia's childhood address on 5th Street. Like Sylvia, he attended Manual High School.

"I was born in the North End of Kansas City, what they call 'Little Italy.' I grew up hanging around the Don Bosco Center and I boxed for them when I was a teenager. I went to Karnes grade school and then I went on to Manual High School. I tell you what, that place was something else in the late 60's. People getting killed down in the basement. Unfortunately, I had to carry a gun to school. It was rough.

"I started working for UPS on February 12, 1979, and on that same day I signed up to become a member of Teamsters Local 41. I was 26 years old.

"You had to complete at least 30 working days to get your seniority and become a member of the union. Like all jobs at UPS, it was hard and challenging work. I was working as a preloader, loading the package cars for the drivers. My start time was 3:00 a.m.

"Most of the management staff were fair and helpful but some supervisors were overaggressive. In my first 30 days, there was one supervisor who followed me into the bathroom every time I went. I spoke with the head shop steward about it, but I had to complete my 30 days before he could take care of the problem, which he did.

"I wanted to know more about the Teamsters, so I read up on the history of the union and learned about Jimmy Hoffa and the Teamsters in Kansas City and other parts of the country. The union did what it had to do to build itself up and to represent the membership. The older Teamsters loved Hoffa. They valued the things he brought to the table. I know about the problems and I know some of them were crooks, but they really took care of the membership. Those days are long gone. Today, violence is nonexistent.

"I became the head shop steward for the Kansas City preload around 1983. I learned contract by reading and asking questions. I spoke with the members, the other stewards, and union leadership. I realized early on that I needed to build relationships with company management and other labor leaders if we were going to be successful. I also had to learn and understand the business side of UPS, so I joined a lot of company committees like the Safety Committee which gave me a greater understanding of the challenges we were up against.

"During the '97 strike, one of the biggest issues were part-time jobs. UPS had way too many part time jobs. They just would not put in full-time jobs. I wrote up three grievances and we won in arbitration, which helped us get more full-time positions.

"I remained head union steward for 26 years until I became a business agent for Local 41 in 2009. As a business agent I was able to travel all over the country and help settle grievances for the membership. I met people in IBT leadership including Jimmy Hoffa Junior. I wrote contracts and I was able to help settle tens-of-thousands of grievances in my career. There were times I was working 17 or 18 hours a day. It was a serious commitment. But I'm not complaining.

"The Teamsters Union is truly a brotherhood and a sisterhood. Leaders and members across the country are always willing to listen and help any way they can. I believe the Teamsters Union is willing to stand up and fight for the working men and women of this country and help preserve the middle class in spite of political challenges.

"The one thing you hate about it is the politics. That's the thing that divides a union, especially during election time. I absolutely hated it, but that's something you can't avoid; you just have to be a part of it.

"I retired from UPS in February of 2020 after 41 years as a Teamster. I still get calls from the members seeking advice and I still help them as best I can because I believe, 'once a Teamster, always a Teamster.'"

Marcello D'Angelo was born in Fasano, Sicily in 1963. When he was 7 months old, he moved with his family to Northeast Kansas City, where he grew up less than a mile from Sylvia's former residence on Independence Avenue.

"I went to work for UPS on August 28, 1996 and joined Local 41 that same day. You don't have to join the union if you work for UPS, but I did and I've been a proud member of the IBT for almost 30 years.

"I love it. They get the employees raises and if you have a problem, the union will fix it. They negotiate a new contract every 5 years. If the company doesn't follow the rules, the union steps in. The pay rate only goes up; it never goes down. The insurance and benefits are outstanding. If a member loses their job, the union will get it back unless that person was guilty of a zero-tolerance violation like stealing, violence, or cheating on their time. One downfall is that sometimes you have an employee who does the bare minimum and isn't a team player and probably doesn't deserve to get their job back, but the union will stand up for them and get it back anyway.

"I love the dual horse head Teamsters logo. It goes back generations and there's a camaraderie that goes with it. If I'm wearing a Teamsters jacket or shirt, some people will still affiliate it with the mob, and if the individual happens to be Italian and looks like me…well, that just makes it worse. But other Teamsters will stop and introduce themselves. Usually it happens in airports, where someone from Chicago or New Jersey or wherever will stop to shake my hand and have a little conversation or maybe sit down and have a beer. There's a lot of tightness. We all stick together for the most part.

"Do you think companies will increase pay and benefits out of the goodness of their hearts? Hell, no. Management can be difficult, cold, standoffish… The 2025 contract is worth about $35 billion over a 5-year period. That's costing the company big money, but the drivers earn it. We're running up to 200 stops a day depending on the route. By ourselves! During peak season you could be doing closer to 300 stops a day, but at least then you have a helper. Try running close to 200 stops a day in the summer without air-conditioning. With this new contract, the union got the company to require all new vehicles to have air-conditioning and increase ventilation in the building.

"In my 29 years, we've only had one strike against UPS. That was in 1997. Jimmy Hoffa Junior was International President then. It lasted a couple of weeks. I walked the picket line right in front of the facility where I worked on North James Street in KCK. The union would give us food and drinks, and if a strike lasts long enough, they pay the strikers a certain amount a week to help make up for lost wages.

"They have meetings almost every Saturday. They have picnics for the family at a park with hot dogs, games and fun, that kind of thing.

"I don't know of any corruption or violence like you had in the old days. There's no violence. There's verbal disagreements, but no fist fighting or anything. They don't tolerate that.

"UPS is a good company. I'm proud to work for them and I'm proud to be a Teamster."

Available where fine books are sold

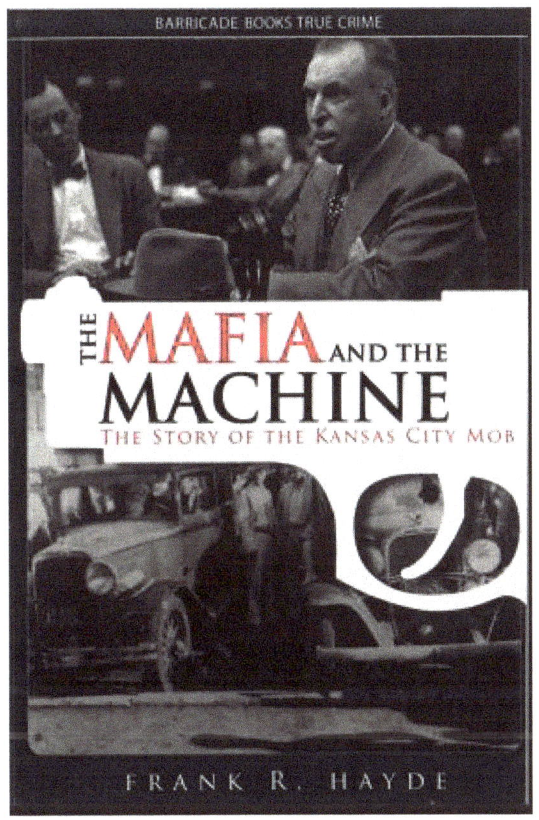

"Frank Hayde presents the mesmerizing true story of the Mafia's influence in Kansas City politics. Infiltration in the police department and the Democratic Party manifested as terror spread on election days. Criminal rackets, eruptions of violence, and other Mafia activity was a daily part of Kansas City life for decades. Efficiently researched and told with a sense of excitement sure to intrigue readers of all backgrounds, The Mafia and the Machine is a highly recommended contribution to American history and criminal history shelves."

Midwest Book Review

"Mafia Dreams" picks up roughly where Hayde's last book, "The Mafia and the Machine," leaves off. The book is difficult to put down. Hayde, much as he did in "The Mafia and the Machine," tells a compelling and riveting tale of the set up and the takedown that ended up making national news and challenging established case law in the process. Here's the bottom line: when you pick this book up, make sure you've got enough time budgeted because this is a compelling work that gets into the meat of the matter on page one and doesn't stop until the last prison door is slammed."

Michael Bushnell, *Northeast News*

ACKNOWLEDGEMENTS

If you missed it earlier, please refer to "Author's Notes" concerning my gratitude to Pat Fasl. This book owes its very existence to his expert assistance. This book would also not have happened without Jack Goldsmith and his book *In Hoffa's Shadow*. And like any author writing about Jimmy Hoffa, I'm indebted to the investigative journalists who have chronicled the Hoffa saga, namely, Scott Burnstein, Dan Moldea, Steven Brill, Jonathan Kwitny, and James Neff.

Chuck O'Brien was kind enough to speak to me and share memories and photographs of his grandmother. Chuck and his wife, Sue, were a joy to converse with on many topics, not just Sylvia.

Thanks to Marcel D'Angelo and James Willis for sharing their insider perspectives as modern Teamsters.

Sue Singleton and Jody Valet provided me with familial and genealogical information. Jody deserves special thanks for her contributions to historic preservation and interpretation in Kansas City, including her latest project, "The Neighborhood: The North End Becomes Columbus Park."

Thanks also to Laurie Purcell of Past to Present Imaging and Margy at Grand Valley Books. There's no order she can't fill, and she always gets the best price. Margy is the quintessential bookseller, and her store is a cornerstone of the community.

SOURCES

Chapter 1: A Brief Introduction to Jimmy Hoffa

- *The Enemy Within* by Robert F. Kennedy. 1960.
- *The Hoffa Wars: Teamsters, Rebels, Politicians and the Mob* by Dan E. Moldea. 1978.
- *In Hoffa's Shadow: A Stepfather, a Disappearance in Detroit, and My Search for the Truth* by Jack Goldsmith. 2019.

Chapter 2: Pueblo and the Legacy of Pellegrino Scaglia

- "Man Arrested Here as Member of New Black Hand." St. Louis Post Dispatch. 08/04/1911
- "Hold Scarred Man in Feud Murder." New York Times 8/5/1911.
- "Scaglia Denies Black Hand Crime, Fights Detention." St. Louis Post Dispatch 8/5/11
- "Detectives Rush Murder Suspect out of Missouri" St. Louis Post Dispatch, 8/30/1911.
- "Black Hand Crimes Doubled in Year Just Ended" New York Times. December 31, 1911.
- "Series of Murders Laid to One Gang" Pueblo Herald-Democrat March 3, 1923 (Mulay and Urso killings)
- Pueblo, Colorado City Directory, 1916.
- *Investigation Concerning Killing of Pellegrino Scaglia, Pueblo, Colorado.* FBI Kansas City Field Office 6/1/1964. KC 92-883 NARA # 124-10287-10202

- *La Cosa Nostra St. Louis Division* FBI file by S.A. Robert L. Bender. 7/23/1964 (Chiapetta/Scaglia/Campo familial relationship)

- *Colorado: Target of Organized Crime. Crooks, Crime, and Colorado*— a report prepared by a task force of the National Council on Crime and Delinquency, early 1970s.

- *Nicola Gentile: Chronicler of early U.S. Mafia History* by Thomas Hunt, editor/publisher of *Informer* - a journal of American crime and law enforcement. October, 2020.

- *Gentile's Pueblo Connection* by Sam Carlino from the journal *Informer.* October, 2020.

- *Vito di Capomafia* by Nicola Gentile. 1963.

- *Mountain Mafia* by Betty K. Alt and Sandra K. Wells. Reprinted 2020.

- *Colorado's Carlino Brothers: A Bootlegging Empire* by Sam Carlino. 2019.

- *In Hoffa's Shadow: A Stepfather, a Disappearance in Detroit, and My Search for the Truth* by Jack Goldsmith. 2019.

- *The Mafia and the Machine: The Story of the Kansas City Mob* by Frank Hayde, 2007.

- *Open City: The True Story of the KC Crime Family* 1900-1950 by William Ouseley. 2008.

Chapter 3: Kansas City

- *Investigation Concerning Killing of Pellegrino Scaglia, Pueblo, Colorado.* FBI Kansas City Field Office 6/1/1964. KC 92-883 NARA # 124-10287-10202

- *La Cosa Nostra St. Louis Division.* FBI file by S.A. Robert L. Bender. 7/23/1964 (Chiapetta/Scaglia/Campo familial relationship)

- *Nicola Gentile: Chronicler of early U.S. Mafia History* by Thomas Hunt, editor and publisher of *Informer* - a journal of American crime and law enforcement.

- Death certificate for infant Sylvia Pagano. Missouri State Board of Health and Vital Statistics, Nov. 19, 1909

- 1957 grand jury testimony of Frank LaRocca in case concerning the purchase of 12 pistols in Gunnison, Colorado.

- Emerson Elementary report cards for Sylvia Pagano

- Manual High yearbooks, 1929-32.

- "Policeman Shot by Young Men in Stolen Auto." St. Louis Post Dispatch, December 7, 1925.

- "Five Boys Flee From House of Detention." St. Louis Post Dispatch, Jan. 25, 1926.

- "25 Year Sentence for By Who Shot Policeman Funke." St. Louis Post Dispatch, April 14, 1926

- FBI memo by Special Agent John L. Shelburne 6/12/1963 NARA # 124-90149-10036. "It should be noted that O'BRIEN had been BINAGGIO'S chauffer prior to his entry into the U.S. Armed Forces in the early 1940's"

- https://katytalescom.wordpress.com/2017/07/18/boonvilles-reformatory-for-boys-1889-1940/

- "Freed in Fatal Raid" Kansas City Star. Sept. 2, 1931. (Lusco flower shop raid and shootout).

- Application for license to marry for Sylvia Pagano and Charles O'Brien. 11/04/1932

- Death certificate for Webster Kemner, 1934

- "Name the Killers." Kansas City Star, March 13, 1934 (Kemner Murder)

- "Phil School Goes Free." Kansas City Star, March 23, 1937

- "Meyer Berman is Held." Kansas City Star, April 9, 1937

- "James Bove is Arrested." Kansas City Star, May 12, 1937 (Carl "Cork" Civella)

- "Robbery, Death in a Quiet Shuffle." Kansas City Star, Feb 17, 1966 (Kemner Murder)

- *Colorado: Target of Organized Crime. Crooks, Crime, and Colorado*— a report prepared by a task force of the National Council on Crime and Delinquency, early 1970s. (Binaggio partnering with the Smaldones).

- U.S. World War II draft card for Charles Linton O'Brien. SN#2498.

- "Cars Kill 2 Men" Kansas City Star, Nov 6, 1941 (Binaggio kills pedestrian).

- Three Bookmakers Pay $420 in Fines," LA Evening Citizen News, Dec. 12, 1946. (Jerome Knoll).

- "Black Mart in New Cars Brings Arrest," Los Angeles Daily News, Nov. 20, 1947. (Jerome Knoll).

- "Auto Black Market Ring Believed Broken By Arrest," LA Evening Citizen News, Nov. 21, 1947. (Jerome Knoll).
- Death certificate for Charles O'Brien with Jerome Knoll as reporting party. June 2, 1947.
- Application for Charles Linton O'Brien's military headstone marker, July 17, 1947.
- "O'Brien Has Deep Roots Here" by John T. Duaner, *The Kansas City Times*, August 8, 1975
- Obituary of Paul Scaglia KC Star, 7/23/2008.
- 1940 Census record for Sylvia O'Brien
- *Vito di Capomafia* by Nicola Gentile. 1963.
- *In Hoffa's Shadow: A Stepfather, a Disappearance in Detroit, and My Search for the Truth* by Jack Goldsmith. 2019.
- *The Mafia and the Machine: The Story of the Kansas City Mob* by Frank Hayde, 2007.
- *Open City: True Story of the KC Crime Family 1900-1950* by William Ouseley, 2008.
- *The Syndicate and the Police: Stories of Law Enforcement Officers Unique Experiences with Members of Organized Crime in Metro-Kansas City.* By Patrick J. Fasl. 2024.
- *The Hoffa Wars: Teamsters, Rebels, Politicians and the Mob* by Dan E. Moldea. 1978. (O'Brein Quote "I'm not a bastard" p.391).

Chapter 4: Detroit

- *The Hoffa Wars: Teamsters, Rebels, Politicians and the Mob* by Dan E. Moldea. 1978.

- *In Hoffa's Shadow: A Stepfather, a Disappearance in Detroit, and My Search for the Truth* by Jack Goldsmith. 2019.
- *The Enemy Within* by Robert F. Kennedy. 1960.
- *Mobsters, Unions and Feds* by James B. Jacobs. 2006.
- *Nicola Gentile: Chronicler of early U.S. Mafia History* by Thomas Hunt, editor/publisher of *Informer* - a journal of American crime and law enforcement. October, 2020. (Frank Coppola).
- *The Brothers Reuther and the Story of the UAW* by Victor G. Reuther. 1976. (Santo Perrone).
- *Motor City Mafia: A Century of Organized Crime in Detroit* by Scott M. Burnstein. 2006.
- FBI file for Frank Coppola (FOIA requested).
- "Teamsters Strike Forces WPA Layoff" *Detroit Evening Times,* May 8, 1941 (Detroit Lumber Company strike).
- Transcripts from the Senate Select Commmittee on Improper Activites in the Labor or Management Field (The McClellan Committee), late 1950's.
- Journalistic notes of Theodore Link of the *Saint Louis Post Dispatch.* National Archive documents avaliable on the Pendergast.org link attached to the Kansas City Public Library's website. (Frank Coppola and Charlie Binaggio).
- Owen "Bert" Brennan obituary, Detroit Free Press, May 1961.
- "Killing Hoffa" film documentary by Scott Burnstein and Al Profit.

Chapter 5: Getting Tight with Hoffa

- *In Hoffa's Shadow: A Stepfather, a Disappearance in Detroit, and My Search for the Truth* by Jack Goldsmith. 2019.
- *The Trials of Jimmy Hoffa, an Autobiography* by James R. Hoffa and Donald I. Rogers. 1970. ("since he was a tot").
- Journalistic notes of Theodore Link, edited into a *Saint Louis Post Dispatch* article that appeared on July 2, 1950. National Archives. (Frank Coppola and Charlie Binaggio).
- *The Strength of the Wolf: The Secret History of America's War on Drugs* by Douglas Valentine. 2006.
- *Where the Mafia Goes to Die* by Pietro Di Donato. Oui Magazine, August, 1974.
- *Open City: The Story of the KC Crime Family 1900-1950* by William Ouseley. 2008.

Chapter 6: Dirty Laundry

- 1950 U.S. Census record for Sylvia O'Brien
- Transcripts from the Select Committee on Improper Activities in the Field of Labor or Management, Eighty-Fifth Congress, First Session, September-Nov, 1957. Part 14. (John Paris and the Laundry Workers).
- Death Certificate of John Paris.
- Obituary of John Paris
- Draft card for John D. Paris SN 00223. Order Number 2708.
- Teamster Magazine, Aug. 1955 (Laundry Workers)
- *Hoffa* by Arthur Sloane. 1993.

- *Mobbed Up: Jackie Presser's High Wire Life in the Teamsters, the Mafia, and the FBI* by James Neff. 1989.
- *Mr. Mob: The Life and Crimes of Moe Dalitz,* by Michael Newton. 2007.
- "Teamsters Official's Home Burned." *Goldsboro News-Argus*, July 17, 1959

Chapter 7: Hoffa Goes National

- *The Hoffa Wars: Teamsters, Rebels, Politicians and the Mob* by Dan E. Moldea. 1978.
- *Dock Boss: Eddie McGrath and the West Side Waterfront* by Neil G. Clark. 2017. (Barney Baker).
- *Vicious Circles: The Mafia in the Marketplace* by Jonathan Kwitny. 1979. (Johnny Dio).
- *In Hoffa's Shadow: A Stepfather, a Disappearance in Detroit, and My Search for the Truth* by Jack Goldsmith. 2019.
- *The Enemy Within:* by Robert F. Kennedy. 1960.
- *Historic Mafia Sit-Downs Vol. 6*, by Scott Burnstein. July 2, 2024. The Gangster Report website https://gangsterreport.com/historic-mafia-sit-downs-vol-5-in-lead-up-to-jimmy-hoffas-iconic-disappearance-detroit-Mob-bosses-giacalone-bros-tried-brokering-peace/ (Red Dorfman from Detroit).

Chapter 8: Work Stoppage

- "O'Brien has Deep Roots Here" by John T. Dauner. *Kansas City Times*, August 8, 1975.

- Report: "Strikes and Racketeering in the Kansas City Area." House Committee on Education and Labor, Special Subcommittee on Strikes and Racketeering, June 29 -July 3, 1953. https://archive.org/details/sim_united-states-congress-hearings-prints-and-reports_1953_8/page/6/mode/2up

- Testimony from House Committee on Education and Labor, Special Subcommittee on Strikes and Racketeering, June 29 -July 3, 1953.

- Affidavit of William N. Ousley, Special Agent, FBI, Kansas City, MO.

- 1985 Deposition of Roy Williams from the President's Commission on Organized Crime, *The Edge: Organized Crime, Business, and Unions.*

- *The Ordeal of Edward Chevlin* by Lester Velie Readers Digest February, 1955

- *The Enemy Within* by Robert F. Kennedy. 1960. (Wint Smith quote p. 52)

- "Shoot at a Union Man" *Kansas City Star*, October 4, 1950. (Lee Quisenberry).

- "Strife in Teamsters Emerges Again" *Kansas City Star* Jan. 30, 1972

- *Open City: True Story of the KC Crime Family 1900-1950* by William Ouseley. 2008.

Chapter 9: Hoffa Versus Kennedy

- *In Hoffa's Shadow: A Stepfather, a Disappearance in Detroit, and My Search for the Truth* by Jack Goldsmith. 2019.

- *Hoffa the Real Story* by James R. Hoffa as told to Oscar Fraley. 1975
- *The Teamsters* by Steven Brill. 1978
- *The Enemy Within:* by Robert F. Kennedy. 1960.
- Various transcripts from the Senate Select Commmittee on Improper Activites in the Labor or Management Field (The McClellan Committee), 1957-58.
- "Flashback: Chuckie O'Brien pounds on this journalist's door after Jimmy Hoffa vanishes" by Jo Thomas *Detroit Free Press* Jan 24, 2024. (Vincent Meli is Chuckie's daughter's godfather).
- https://gangsterreport.com/longtime-detroit-Mob-chieftain-tony-giacalone-made-his-bones-with-1948-double-homicide-informant-told-feds/

Chapter 10: The Fund

- *Leaving Vegas: The True Story of How the FBI Wiretaps Ended Mob Domination of Las Vegas Casinos* by Gary Jenkins 2016.
- *The Teamsters* by Steven Brill. 1978
- *Mobbed Up: Jackie Presser's High Wire Life in the Teamsters, the Mafia, and the FBI* by James Neff. 1989.
- JFK Assassination System Files; electronic surveillance (ELSUR) documents and transcripts from the FBI's "June" file from illegal FBI microphones at Sylvia's apartment and Tony Giacalone's business. Jan. 1961-1964. Available on the Mary Ferrell Foundation website.

Chapter 11: Nick Civella Get's His Way

- "Strife in Teamsters Emerges Again" *Kansas City Star* Jan. 30, 1972
- *The Mafia and the Machine: The Story of the Kansas City Mob* by Frank Hayde, 2007.
- *Open City: The True Story of the KC Crime Family* 1900-1950 by William Ouseley. 2008.
- *Mobsters in Our Midst: The Kansas City Crime Family* by William Ouseley. 2011.

Chapter 12 Arson and Surveillance

- JFK Assassination System Files; electronic surveillance (ELSUR) documents and transcripts from the FBI's "June" file from illegal FBI microphones at Sylvia's apartment and Tony Giacalone's business. Jan. 1961-1964. Available on the Mary Ferrell Foundation website.
- FBI FOIA file on Anthony Giacalone, 1959. (Arson at Sylvia's house etc.)
- Immigration and Naturalization Service reports on Sylvia Paris from 1963-64. (Cash and jewelry stolen by arsonist).
- INS Mail Cover for Sylvia Pagano 1964. (LaSalle Distributing and French perfume).
- "Set Afire by Two Men" *The Kansas City Times,* Aug 05, 1958
- "Kierdorf Spent His Life Playing with Fire" *Newsday,* Aug 05, 1958

- "Arsonists Start Fire in Teamster's Home" *The Ogden Standard-Examiner.* July 17, 1959

- "Secret Clues Show How Own Bomb Slew Kierdorf." *Detroit Free Press,* 8/8/1958

- "Blaze Destroys Teamster's Home" *Ironwood Daily Globe.* July 17, 1959

- "Home of Teamster Burns: Arson Seen" *Lubbock Avalanche-Journal* July 18, 1959.

- "Police Probing Arson Clues as Temasters's Home Burns" *Ann Arbor News,* July 18, 1959

- "Detectives Quiz Oil Dealers in Fire at Teamster Home." *Detroit Free Press* July 19, 1959.

- "Insurance Firms Charge Arson in Home Blaze." *Holland Evening Sentinel,* Feb 9, 1960

- *All American Mafioso: The Johnny Roselli Story* by Charles Rappleye and Ed Becker. 1991. (Cuba).

- *Mobbed Up: Jackie Presser's High Wire Life in the Teamsters, the Mafia, and the FBI* by James Neff. 1989. (Cuba).

Chapter 13: Sylvia's Slugger Son

- *The Hoffa Wars: Teamsters, Rebels, Politicians and the Mob* by Dan E. Moldea. 1978.

- *Hoffa the Real Story* by James R. Hoffa as told to Oscar Fraley. 1975

- *Mob Lawyer: Including the Inside Account of Who Killed Jimmy Hoffa and JFK.* By Frank Ragano and Selwyn Raab. 1994

- JFK Assassination System Files; electronic surveillance (ELSUR) documents and transcripts from the FBI's

"June" file from illegal FBI microphones at Sylvia's apartment and Tony Giacalone's business. Jan. 1961-1964. Available on the Mary Ferrell Foundation website.

Chapter 14: "I'll Take Care of Everything."

- Death certificate and obituary for Jospeh Pagano.
- "Charge 3 in Theft of Ship Salvage" Detroit Free Press March 22, 1963.
- "Hoffa Aide Guilty in Theft of Montrose Cargo" Detroit Free Press, Dec. 25, 1964.
- "Salvage Robbers Sentenced" Detroit Free Press, June 18, 1965.
- "Auto Bomb Injures Gangster Perrone" Detroit Free Press, Jan. 20, 1964.
- *In Hoffa's Shadow: A Stepfather, a Disappearance in Detroit, and My Search for the Truth* by Jack Goldsmith. 2019.
- *The Enemy Within:* by Robert F. Kennedy. 1960.
- *The Grim Reapers: The Anatomy of Organized Crime in America, City by City,* by Ed Reid. 1969. (Perrone bombings).
- JFK Assassination System Files; electronic surveillance (ELSUR) documents and transcripts from the FBI's "June" file from illegal FBI microphones at Sylvia's apartment and Tony Giacalone's business. Jan. 1961-1964. Available on the Mary Ferrell Foundation website.
- FBI FOIA file on Anthony Giacalone, 1959. (Provenzano's testimonial dinner).

- Various transcripts from the Senate Select Commmittee on Improper Activites in the Labor or Management Field (The McClellan Committee), 1957-58.
- INS Mail Cover for Sylvia Pagano 1964. (LaSalle Distributing and French perfume).
- Federal Trade Commission Memorandium of Decisions, Jan-August, 1965 (LaSalle Distributing Company).
- "Teamster Accused in Stoning." *Detroit Free Press,* Nov 10, 1960.
- "Hoffa Aide Warrants Held Up." *Detroit Free Press,* April 30, 1961.
- *Motor City Mafia: A Century of Organized Crime in Detroit,* by Scott Burnstein. 2006.
- *The Teamsters* by Steven Brill. 1978
- *Heroin and the 20th Century Detroit Mafia,* by Scott Burnstein   https://gangsterreport.com/heroin-the-20th-century-detroit-mafia/
- Original Gangsters Podcast by Scott Burnstein: various episodes on Jimmy Hoffa (Hoffa brought Provenzano into the Teamsters).

Chapter 15: Assassination and Immigration

- *In Hoffa's Shadow: A Stepfather, a Disappearance in Detroit, and My Search for the Truth* by Jack Goldsmith. 2019.
- *Mafia Kingfish: Carlos Marcello and the Assassination of John F. Kennedy* by John H. Davis. 1988.

- JFK Assassination System Files; electronic surveillance (ELSUR) documents from the FBI's "June" file from illegal FBI microphones at Sylvia's apartment and Tony Giacalone's business. Jan. 1961-1964. Available on the Mary Ferrell Foundation website.

- Immigration and Naturalization Service reports on Sylvia Paris from 1963-64.

- FBI FOIA file on Anthony Giacalone, 1959.

- Detroit FBI memo from Special Agent John L. Shelburne, 6/12/1963. NARA record number 124-90149-10036.

- *I Heard You Paint Houses*, by Charles Brandt. 2004 (Reference to Moldea's postscript from *The Hoffa Wars* describing Hoffa's association with Jack Ruby).

Chapter 16: Stealing Money From Hoffa

- JFK Assassination System Files; electronic surveillance (ELSUR) documents and transcripts from the FBI's "June" file from illegal FBI microphones at Sylvia's apartment and Tony Giacalone's business. Jan. 1961-1964. Available on the Mary Ferrell Foundation website.

- *In Hoffa's Shadow: A Stepfather, a Disappearance in Detroit, and My Search for the Truth* by Jack Goldsmith. 2019.

- *The Life We Chose: William "Big Billy D'Elia and the Last Secrets of America's Most Powerful Mafia Family* by Matt Birkbeck. 2023.

- *Mob Lawyer: Including the Inside Account of Who Killed Jimmy Hoffa and JFK.* By Frank Ragano and Selwyn Raab. 1994

- *Mobbed Up: Jackie Presser's High Wire Life in the Teamsters, the Mafia, and the FBI* by James Neff. 1989. (Jukebox local, etc.).
- *Vicious Circles: The Mafia in the Marketplace* by Jonathan Kwitny. 1979. (Quote from Missouri driver).

Chapter 17: Hoffa Goes to Prison

- *In Hoffa's Shadow: A Stepfather, a Disappearance in Detroit, and My Search for the Truth* by Jack Goldsmith. 2019.
- *Hoffa the Real Story* by James R. Hoffa as told to Oscar Fraley. 1975
- *Mob Lawyer: Including the Inside Account of Who Killed Jimmy Hoffa and JFK.* By Frank Ragano and Selwyn Raab. 1994
- *The Teamsters* by Steven Brill. 1978
- *Vicious Circles: The Mafia in the Marketplace* by Jonathan Kwitny. 1979. (Johnny Dio).

Chapter 18: Sylvia's Death.

- JFK Assassination System Files; electronic surveillance (ELSUR) documents and transcripts from the FBI's "June" file from illegal FBI microphones at Sylvia's apartment and Tony Giacalone's business. Jan. 1961-1964. Available on the Mary Ferrell Foundation website.
- Obituary of Sylvia Paris.

- *In Hoffa's Shadow: A Stepfather, a Disappearance in Detroit, and My Search for the Truth* by Jack Goldsmith. 2019. P. 303-4
- Phone interviews with Sylvia's grandson, Chuck O'Brien, 2025.

Chapter 19: Post Prison Power Struggle

- FBI "Hoffex" Memo January 27-8, 1976.
- *Historic Mafia Sit-Downs Vol. 6*, by Scott Burnstein. July 2, 2024. The Gangster Report website https://gangsterreport.com/historic-mafia-sit-downs-vol-5-in-lead-up-to-jimmy-hoffas-iconic-disappearance-detroit-Mob-bosses-giacalone-bros-tried-brokering-peace/
- *In Hoffa's Shadow: A Stepfather, a Disappearance in Detroit, and My Search for the Truth* by Jack Goldsmith. 2019. P. 303-4
- *Hoffa's Man: The Rise and Fall of Jimmy Hoffa as Witnessed by His Strongest Arm,* by Joe with Richard Hammer. 1987. Pg. 295.
- *Mobbed Up: Jackie Presser's High Wire Life in the Teamsters, the Mafia, and the FBI* by James Neff. 1989.
- *Mob Lawyer: Including the Inside Account of Who Killed Jimmy Hoffa and JFK.* By Frank Ragano and Selwyn Raab. 1994
- *The Life We Chose: William "Big Billy D'Elia and the Last Secrets of America's Most Powerful Mafia Family* by Matt Birkbeck. 2023.

Chapter 20: Disappearance

- FBI "Hoffex" Memo January 27-8, 1976.
- *The Hoffa Hit Timeline: What Exactly Happened the Day the Teamsters Boss Died* by Scott Burnstein. The Gangster Report website, July 30, 2015
- *Mob Lawyer: Including the Inside Account of Who Killed Jimmy Hoffa and JFK.* By Frank Ragano and Selwyn Raab. 1994
- *The Hoffa Wars: Teamsters, Rebels, Politicians and the Mob* by Dan E. Moldea. 1978.
- *In Hoffa's Shadow: A Stepfather, a Disappearance in Detroit, and My Search for the Truth* by Jack Goldsmith. 2019.
- *Mobbed Up: Jackie Presser's High Wire Life in the Teamsters, the Mafia, and the FBI* by James Neff. 1989.
- "Killing Hoffa" film documentary by Scott Burnstein and Al Profit.

Epilogue

- "Roy Lee Williams, the Mob and the Teamsters" by Michael Yablonsky, *The Kansas City Star*, June 1, 1981.
- 1985 Deposition of Roy Williams from the President's Commission on Organized Crime, *The Edge: Organized Crime, Business, and Unions.*
- *The Hoffa Wars: Teamsters, Rebels, Politicians and the Mob* by Dan E. Moldea. 1978.
- *Mobbed Up: Jackie Presser's High Wire Life in the Teamsters, the Mafia, and the FBI* by James Neff. 1989.
- *Striving: Adventures of a Female Journalist in a Man's World* by Jo Thomas. 2023.

- "Flashback: Chuckie O'Brien pounds on this journalist's door after Jimmy Hoffa vanishes" by Jo Thomas *Detroit Free Press* Jan 24, 2024.
- "The Lost Suspect: Detroit Mafia Steel Baron "Little Vince" Meli Was Second-In-Command In Hoffa Murder Conspiracy" by Scott Burnstein in Gansterreport.com. July 30, 2024
- Telephone interviews with Chuck O'Brien (Sylvia's grandson)

AUTHOR'S BIO

Frank R. Hayde is a career law enforcement officer whose Kansas City heritage reaches back to the 19th century. Descended from Irish-American bricklayers and machine politicians, he brings a deep personal connection to the city's colorful past and its ties to organized crime.

Hayde is the author of several other books including: *The Mafia and the Machine: The Story of the Kansas City Mob; Mafia Dreams: A True Crime Saga of Young Men at the End of an Era in Kansas City; Stan Levy: Jazz Heavyweight; and Italian Gardens: A History of Kansas City Through Its Favorite Restaurant.*